home
groups

the everything-you-need-to-know guide

Housegroups are one of the few places in church life where you can press the red button and go interactive! So this practical resource on running them is most welcome.

Rob Lacey, author

Just because homegroups take place in the home there is a natural tendency to believe that running one is as easy as hosting any social gathering of friends. The Briars have brought great insight, gentle humor, good examples, a sense of practicality, and above all, solutions. A task that will be carried out with far greater ease and success as an enriching experience for the leader if every pearl of the wisdom in this book is absorbed and applied to this challenging and rewarding experience.

Gospatric Home, Chairman CRE

This is a guide for homegroup leaders and organizers that is intensely practical and pulls no punches. The Briars will keep you entertained while you read alright, but don't expect them to let you get away with any lazy, fluffy practices! Their guide is Bible-centered but contains all sorts of hints, directions, warnings, and examples from contemporary practice, including guidance on Bible study aids and templates of forms. If you're involved with leading or organizing homegroups, you'll want to send the Briars flowers in gratitude for this encyclopedia/recipe book.

Conrad Gempf

A key component to a healthy church is a homegroup—Steve Briars' book is a timely arrival, to help us reshape and re-envision us in creating healthy groups that will produce growth, spiritually and numerically—I urge all homegroup leaders to PLEASE read this book.

J. John, author

In a fragmented and relationally depleted society, small groups are one of the foundational building blocks of twenty-first century church.

Homegroups, full of wisdom, ideas, and practical insight, should be viewed as essential reading for anyone wanting to begin or develop a homegroup ministry within their congregation.

Rev. Chris Stoddard, Director of RUN
(Reaching the Unchurched Network)

homegroups

the everything-you-need-to-know guide

Steve and Mandy Briars

COLORADO SPRINGS · LONDON · HYDERABAD

Authentic Publishing

We welcome your questions and comments.

USA   1820 Jet Stream Drive, Colorado Springs, CO 80921
       www.authenticbooks.com

UK   9 Holdom Avenue, Bletchley, Milton Keynes, Bucks, MK1 1QR
       www.authenticmedia.co.uk

India Logos Bhavan, Medchal Road, Jeedimetla Village, Secunderabad 500 055, A.P.

Homegroups

ISBN-13: 978-1-934068-07-6

ISBN-10: 1-934068-07-1

Cover design: Paul Lewis

Interior design: Angela Lewis

Editorial team: Dana Carrington, KJ Larson

Printed in the United States of America

With special thanks to Simon and Adel,
Mark, Lizzie, and Charlie, our family.

Jane Young and Kim Nourse for all their help and support.

All the people who have made the writing of this book possible,
even if they never know it.

This book is dedicated to the memory of

REVEREND TERRY PEASLEY

Terry Peasley was senior pastor at Southcourt Baptist Church, Aylesbury for twenty-three years before his sudden death in September 2004. He had retired only eighteen months earlier.

Terry first introduced homegroups to Southcourt in the early 1980s, a new concept for the church and one that grew under his leadership. Over the years, the number of homegroups grew to the current twenty-one, with two hundred sixty people attending and over sixty leaders. He also introduced the idea of homegroup pastors, with ten now actively caring for the homegroups at Southcourt.

Terry was a man who dearly loved his Lord and prayed longingly for people to come to a personal faith. He was a warm, friendly person with a great sense of humor.

Mandy and I were privileged to work with Terry and he became a good friend. Without his ministry this book would not have been written.

CONTENTS

PART 3: TEACHING IN HOMEGROUPS

PART 4: ORGANIZING HOMEGROUPS

FOREWORD

Homegroups. We either love them or hate them, but it's almost universally accepted that to do church well, we need to have them. Okay, there are challenges. Maybe Doris insists on giving an update on her lumbago every week (complete with x-ray charts) and young Henry the zealot uses every homegroup meeting as an opportunity to berate everyone for not handing out tracts to the Saturday morning shoppers in town. And Bill gets healed of insomnia every week, judging by his snoring.

But not only is small group life vital—we will need to invest in the homegroup to make sure that it is a creative, equipping event. The main word used in the New Testament to describe the Christian is "disciple"—pupil, learner. That's only going to be a reality as we learn together. And more than that, it's great to come in from the cold and, in the homegroup, huddle together for warmth and strength.

So I welcome this practical, accessible, and punchy book by Steve and Mandy Briars. They are practitioners, not armchair theorists; in these pages you will find countless nuggets that will shine as you determine to make that small group the best it can be.

Perhaps Tuesday night is homegroup night; you're the leader, and Tuesday cometh. Well, stop reading this foreword now. Get on with this great book.

Jeff Lucas
Author, speaker, broadcaster

A PERSONAL NOTE

Dear homegroup leader,

How can we best describe *Homegroups: The Everything-you-Need-To-Know Guide*? Probably not as a textbook. Nor is it a workbook. Is it a guide? The *Oxford Dictionary* defines the word "guide" as "one who shows the way" which neatly sums up what *Homegroups: The Everything-you-Need-To-Know Guide* sets out to be. This book is based on our twenty-five years experience of leading and organizing homegroups and covers everything from the practicalities of leading worship to organizing social activities. It has been written in an easy-to-read style and includes stories of our family and the many people we have shared homegroups with over the years.

The book has been laid out in four parts:

Part 1: Introduction to homegroups

Are homegroups still relevant in a rapidly changing church culture? What can they achieve? Who are they for? This section will try to answer these questions.

Part 2: Caring for homegroups

Don't be surprised when you read this section if you identify with some of the stories. This is the hands-on part that is honest and practical and looks at everything from pastoral care to over-amorous dogs!

Part 3: Teaching in homegroups

Do you sometimes find praying together in the homegroup difficult? Does the Bible study seem dull and the worship flat? In this section we will look at a few of the reasons why and offer some practical solutions.

Part 4: Organizing homegroups

A must-read section for all church leaders who are involved in organizing and overseeing homegroups. Honest, down to earth, practical advice on how to structure homegroups, train leaders, and much more.

By all means feel free to dip into the book and read the sections that appeal to you most. However, our recommendation would be to read the book from cover to cover, which will help you to see the big picture of homegroups. This is not a workbook, so there are no questions for you to answer or pages for you to complete. Nevertheless, we would encourage you to read this book with one question in mind at all times: "Is there at least one thing I can take from *Homegroups* and put into practice that would enhance my homegroup ministry?"

We hope you enjoy reading this book as much as we have enjoyed writing it.

Your co-homegroup leaders

Steve & Mandy Briars

PART 1:

INTRODUCTION TO HOMEGROUPS

CHAPTER 1

WHY HOMEGROUPS?

1.1   A biblical model

There is clear biblical evidence both in the Old and New Testaments that small groups are the best way in which to manage both the administration and care of a large number of people. Meeting in small groups is therefore not a new idea—the book of Exodus records how Moses and his father-in-law Jethro divided the nation of Israel into manageable groups (Exodus 18:13–26). Jesus began his earthly ministry by choosing the disciples—those twelve men who became the most spoken and written about small group in all of history (Matthew 4:18–22, Luke 6:13–16). Luke, in the book of Acts, tells how the believers met in each other's homes for prayer (Acts 12:12), teaching (Acts 20:7), and fellowship (Acts 21:7). Gathering together in homes became common for the early Christians, a place where they shared their faith in a risen Lord Jesus. Their lifestyle was such a powerful witness that new believers joined them daily.

Neal F. McBride in his book, *How to Lead Small Groups[1]* writes

> The small group ministry is founded on a rock-hard biblical base. This firm foundation guards against the storms of change brought about by the many programmatic fads that blow through our churches. Although initially these fads seem exciting and potentially beneficial, they quickly subside because they lack a clear biblical basis. Small groups are not one of these fanciful fads. In fact, of all the potential ministry formats available to the local church, *small groups have the greatest biblical support!* Consequently, it is important for you as a small group leader to understand and appreciate the rich biblical heritage that precedes you.

Nearly two thousand years have elapsed since those pioneering Christians in Jerusalem first gathered in homes to share their faith. Undeniably, we live in a vastly different time and culture, but we are the benefactors of their timeless blueprint.

---

1. Neal McBride, *How to Lead Small Groups* (Navpress: 1990).

1.2   A case for homegroups

Are homegroups, therefore, still relevant? They are not a new concept and have been around for many years, so do they still meet needs in today's culture and emerging church? We believe that the church should not stand still; we have to be innovative to reach people for God's kingdom and to care for those who are already part of it. On the other hand, we should not throw out the baby with the bath water. If something which has been around for a while is still working and still necessary, it should not be discarded. Homegroups are one such case. They may not be new, but in fact the need for them is increasing, not diminishing.

Homegroups offer a balanced approach to the care and spiritual development of both new and mature Christians. They can be inward rather than outward looking, and sometimes it is argued that they spend too much time nurturing believers when their priority should be seeking people who are outside the kingdom. It is not a case of either/or; both are important. As we grow in our faith, we will naturally want to share what we believe with others. Homegroups can be part of our evangelism and can help us to do it.

Over the past few years the church has adopted two words, "community" and "fellowship." These need to be more than just words used in our church language; they have to become part of our Christian lifestyle. Increasingly, we find ourselves speaking to Christians who have made a conscious decision to stop attending church; not because of their lack of faith but simply because they do not feel part of the church community and lack close fellowship with other Christians. It is an accepted fact that it is difficult, if not impossible, to get to know more than about fifty or sixty people in a church, regardless of its size, and even then we won't know all of them that well. It is one thing to be associated with a community; it is something altogether different to have friendships within that community. While this is obvious, it is worth emphasizing: the more friendships people have within the church, the less likely they are to leave.

Friendships, rather than the quality of preaching, are often the reason why individuals continue to attend a particular church. Fellowship with other Christians should not be viewed as an optional extra; it is not like buying a car where we have the choice between the basic model or upgrading to add the extra bells and whistles. The need for fellowship with others is not an add-on; it is a basic requirement for mankind. We get very distressed when we read statistics on the number of people in this country who are leaving the church. We are not suggesting that homegroups are the panacea for all the church's problems. However, caring for people in homegroups is one way you can help prevent them slipping out of the back door without anyone ever noticing.

Building lasting relationships within the church, then, is a key reason for having homegroups, but there are many more reasons why good homegroups benefit both the individuals in them and the wider church.

> A person standing alone can be attacked and defeated,
> but two can stand back-to-back and conquer. Three are
> even better, for a triple-braided cord is not easily broken.
> (Ecclesiastes 4:12)

1.3　What is the purpose of homegroups?

This question is more complex to answer than would first appear because it is hard to encapsulate in a few brief sentences. We cannot purely build a case for homegroups only around the importance of community and fellowship. Yes, the need for a sense of community is important, however there are other reasons why homegroups have an essential role in the life of the church today. For example, we are rapidly becoming an illiterate biblical culture, where our knowledge of what is new and hot in the latest Christian praise and worship songs is often greater than our knowledge of God's word. Often the level of biblical comprehension for many Christians is now fairly basic, and fewer and fewer people are reading their Bibles on a daily basis—a disappointing fact, but nevertheless true. To imply homegroups are the one-stop solution to this concern would be an inappropriate sweeping statement, but homegroups are possibly the only place where some Christians regularly read their Bibles and have the opportunity to talk about how they can apply its truths.

A place to study God's word and fellowship are important, but they need to be viewed as only part of the argument why homegroups still remain a vital ministry. Yet to define a homegroup as a group of people who meet regularly for the purpose of Bible study and prayer would be only partially true. Equally, to describe them as places where friends can meet for coffee and chat is also partially true. What then is the purpose of homegroups? We would describe them as a place where spiritual and social needs can be met within a caring environment.

We therefore believe there are at least nine reasons why homegroups continue to meet the ministry needs of many churches today. These nine reasons or principles are:

To study God's word

Studying the Bible together will help us to understand its meaning and apply it to our lives.

> Study this Book of the Law continually. Meditate on
> it day and night so you may be sure to obey all that is
> written in it. Only then will you succeed. (Joshua 1:8)

To apply God's word

Understanding God's word is important; applying it to our lives is essential. Homegroups will help us achieve both.

And remember, it is a message to obey, not just to listen to. If you don't obey, you are only fooling yourself. (James 1:22)

To pray together

Prayer brings us closer to God; praying together brings us closer to one another.

The Lord is close to all who call on him, yes, to all who call on him sincerely. (Psalm 145:18)

To worship God

"Worship is loving God in the presence of one another and loving one another in the presence of God" (source unknown).

Everything on earth will worship you; they will sing your praises, shouting your name in glorious songs. (Psalm 66:4).

To practice spiritual gifts

Spiritual gifts are from God and should be used to bless and encourage each other.

God has given gifts to each of you from his great variety of spiritual gifts. Manage them well so that God's generosity can flow through you. (1 Peter 4:10)

To be a witness to others

Share Jesus' love and gift of salvation to everyone.

> And he told them, "Go into the world and preach the
> Good News to everyone, everywhere." (Mark 16:15)

To nurture friendships

Friendships are essential for all of us. They should be encouraged
to grow and blossom through the homegroup.

> There are "friends" who destroy each other, but real
> friends stick closer than a brother. (Proverbs 18:24)

To share Christian fellowship

As we share fellowship, we build relationships that are building
and strengthening the church.

> We who believe are carefully joined together, becoming a
> holy temple for the Lord. (Ephesians 2:21)

To care for one another

Caring is seeking to offer practical assistance, bringing healing
and wholeness in the name of Jesus Christ.

> This makes for harmony among the members, so that all
> members care for each other equally.
> (1 Corinthians 12:25)

We have deliberately refrained from numbering the above list or
writing them in any order of importance. Please do not misunderstand
what we are saying; Bible study and prayer are essential for the well-
being of the group. Conversely do not neglect the need for worship,

friendship, and care for they are equally important. A homegroup should be a place where we can support and encourage each other so that we may grow strong in our Christian faith and be a witness to others.

1.4   Who are homegroups for?

The answer to this will help to determine the purpose and direction for your homegroup ministry. Who are homegroups for? Are they for regular members of the church who are committed Christians, or is it broader than that? Should homegroups be open to non-believers so they can attend and hear the Gospel? As you might have already surmised the answer is not clear-cut, one or the other; both are important. But does that mean there is a danger of the group having no clearly defined direction? There is a saying, "Aim at nothing and you are certain to hit it." It is therefore important for homegroups to have a clear under-standing of who they are there for. First of all, you should identify the potential groups of people that could attend or be associated with your group. Are they:

- Christians who regularly attend church?
- Christian spouses of group members who do not regularly attend the group?
- non-Christian spouses of group members?
- immediate family of group members?
- non-Christian friends and neighbors?

This is not an exhaustive list but probably identifies the main groupings. The question now is what are our priorities? Is it as easy as dropping a few percentage points against each group? For example, should 10 percent of the life of the homegroup be devoted to non-Christian friends and neighbors? The fact—it's not a numbers game.

From my experience, groups go through different seasons, due to the mix of people that attend. Maybe the group consists predominantly of young, Christian, married couples who are regular members and whose immediate family are not nearby. In this case the main emphasis should be on caring and nurturing these young couples and also encouraging them to share their faith with non-Christian friends and neighbors through the homegroup. Then, again, the focus will change with a different mix of people. Does this mean homegroups are first and foremost inward looking? Hopefully not! However, there has to be a starting point and it should be the needs of the Christians who attend the group. Now begin to broaden your horizons to those you know and already have contact with: family, friends, and neighbors. In other words, it may be possible to divide the homegroups' yearly cycle so that all associated groups are taken into account. Perhaps the answer is that different people and seasons will bring different needs that help keep homegroups refreshing and rewarding.

1.5   A place to witness

If homegroups, as we have already established, should be open to those outside the church, then how are we going to do this? What sort of outreach is appropriate for a homegroup to be involved in?

Bill Hybels and Mark Mittelberg, in their book *Becoming a Contagious Christian*[2] write,

> We are on a mission. Deep in every true Christian, there is an awareness that we are on this planet for purposes greater than having a career, paying the bills, loving our families, and fulfilling our role as upstanding citizens. Even going

---

2.   Bill Hybels and Mark Mittelberg, *Becoming a Contagious Christian* (Zondervan: 1996).

to church and worshipping God—important as these are—
sometimes leave us feeling that something is missing. After
all, we'll worship God for eternity in heaven; we don't have
to be here to do that. What is it that's absent in the lives of
so many believers who are crying out for fulfillment? What
on earth is God asking us to do?

God wants us to become contagious Christians—his
agents, who will first catch his love and then urgently and
infectiously offer it to all who are willing to consider it. This
is his primary plan, the one Jesus modeled so powerfully, to
spread God's grace and truth person to person until there's
an epidemic of changed lives around the world.

Who of us would not raise a hearty "amen" to these words from
Hybels and Mittelberg as they encourage us to become contagious
(infectious) witnesses? Jesus' own words in the Gospel of Mark leave
us in no doubt of our responsibility,

Go into all the world and preach the good news to
everyone, everywhere. (Mark 16:15)

Why then do so few groups actively get involved in any form of
evangelistic outreach? Throughout our involvement with homegroups
we have come across very few that have moved beyond the theory of
witnessing to putting it into practice. The problem is not the lack of
good intentions but simply not knowing what to do. This reminds me
of my school reports that invariably ended with a note from my teacher
that read, "Stephen needs to try harder." I always thought this entirely
missed the point. The lack of academic achievement was not attributed
to laziness on my part but rather an inability to understand the subject.
I needed enlightenment rather than criticism. When it comes to evangelism, for most homegroups it is not a case of "needs to try harder"
but simply the lack of direction or know-how. Acknowledging the
problem is one thing; doing something about it is something else. The

dilemma for most homegroups is not the question of who to witness to, but rather, how?

Witnessing needs to begin with people you already have a relationship with. As we have already mentioned, you need look no further than family, friends, and neighbors. This is not to imply witnessing through homegroups should be restricted to these three groups. It is just that although you should have a global vision, in reality most of us are only able to influence people who you have regular contact with. You need to understand that unless time is set aside for witnessing in the homegroup program, it will never happen. This is not to limit God but to help us, both as a homegroup and individuals, put into practice what so many of us find difficult to achieve on a daily basis. Our concern is that you never advance beyond good intentions or, at the very best, consider that inviting people to a barbecue constitutes evangelism. It is important for groups to move from verbally accepting that it has a responsibility to witness to non-believers, to the point of actively doing something about it. The question is how? We appreciate no two homegroups are the same and therefore the "how" will vary from group to group; nevertheless, there are a few principles that will help in the developing of an outreach program.

Is everyone on board?

It is probably not the wisest or most sensitive approach to spring upon your group that for the next few weeks they have to bring their next-door neighbor along, though if nothing else, you would have everyone's attention! Instead, over a period of time, introduce the idea that it would be good to hold a few special events where they could invite non-Christian friends and family. Try to avoid giving the impression this is an imposed decision and that everyone *has* to bring someone. It would be good if they did but probably it won't happen; however you do want the entire group to be supportive of the idea.

How often?

Frequency probably doesn't matter much; but it does matter that the when, where, and how often are fixed in advance, otherwise evangelism will remain a good intention for your homegroup but won't actually happen. It is better to do something twice a year and do it well, rather than over-commit yourself and end up feeling defeated.

What to do?

Are you almost embarrassed to share with other people what you believe? We include ourselves in this. Is an invitation to simply join the homegroup too straightforward? Do you really know if your next-door neighbor would be offended or pleased to join the group? Admittedly, this may not be the best approach for everyone, and it is probably best to invite people to a social event that they would find interesting. For example, if you know someone who has been involved in overseas relief work and is willing to share his experiences with your group, this could be an ideal opportunity to invite non-Christians. Alternatively, an evening watching the DVD of *The Passion of Christ* could be an interesting way to introduce a person to our Lord. Social events, such as quizzes, going bowling, having a meal, or anything that won't be viewed as taking someone out of her comfort zone into yours might be good. Whatever you do, it needs to be viewed as first base only. How you progress will depend upon the individual. It is good to have ideas of what else you could invite them to, perhaps a special service at the church such as at Christmas or Easter—people who are not usually comfortable with church will often be happy coming to sing carols, where they can be fairly sure of knowing both the words and the tune! Whatever you do, do not see this as a one-time invitation. Most people require time, perhaps many months or even years, to reach a point where they can make a commitment.

Just a thought

Within the context of a few paragraphs, it is difficult to outline a comprehensive outreach program, and to do so properly would take another book. However, if nothing else, the question has been raised as to why homegroups need to be a place for witnessing. Both group leaders and church leaders should be encouraged to ensure time is regularly allotted for evangelism through homegroups. We imagine many of you are reading this book because someone first took the time and trouble to introduce you to Jesus.

1.6   The Holy Spirit and homegroups

A few weeks ago, while tidying my office, we came across the original handwritten notes for the outline of this book. They made for fascinating reading. What started out as a kernel of an idea has now turned into a finished book. As we scrolled down the list, almost everything was there from how to care for your group to how to organize a social event. However, what we could not find was any reference to the work of the Holy Spirit in homegroups. It would appear in our initial haste to write down what we perceived as essential for a book on running homegroups, we had left out the most important, the work and ministry of the Holy Spirit. You should not forget that the Holy Spirit is not only the unseen present member of the group but that you are his co-leader. Our role is to facilitate, leading and caring for the group under his direction. Neil McBride, in his book, *How to Lead Small Groups,* refers to the seven ministries of the Holy Spirit in a small group:

He indwells: Romans 8:9–11

He guides: John 16:13

He teaches:	John 14:26
He convicts:	John 16:8
He intercedes:	Romans 8:26
He enables:	1 Corinthians 12:11
He unifies:	Ephesians 4:3

We have no doubt that God's desire is for us to be open to the working of the Holy Spirit in our homegroups and to do more than acknowledge his presence, we also need to live in his presence. Joel Comiskey, of Cell Church Solutions[3] explains there are four key principles to discovering how to use gifts within a small group environment.

1. Find out about spiritual gifts by reading the relevant Bible passages (1 Corinthians 12, Romans 12, Ephesians 4).

2. In the small group try to exercise as many gifts as possible, both speaking and serving gifts.

3. Discover what each other person would like to do. Exercising a gift should not be a chore. You should enjoy it. Does someone like explaining Bible truth? Perhaps he has the gift of teaching. Does someone else enjoy praying for people in the group and seeing them healed? Perhaps she has the gift of healing. Does another individual love to bring refreshments and organize group events? Perhaps he has the gift of helping. Is anyone drawn to visit a group member who is having problems? Perhaps she has the gift of encouragement.

4. Look for confirmation from those in the group. People will be edified by each other's gifts. Ask for their opinions. What do they confirm? Do they notice someone's capacity to clarify the meaning of Scripture; it's likely that person has the gift of

---

3. Joel Comiskey, *Spiritual Gifts and Small Group Life*, (extract from an article on the internet from Cell Church Solutions, USA, 2004)

teaching. Often others can spot gifts that we are not aware of, so get everyone involved in helping each other to know what their gifts are.

The apostle Peter teaches:

> God has given gifts to each of you from the great variety of spiritual gifts. Manage them well so that God's generosity can flow through you. Are you called to be a speaker? Then speak as though God himself were speaking through you. Are you called to help others? Do it with all the strength and energy that God supplies. Then God will be given the glory in everything through Jesus Christ. All glory and power belong to him forever and ever. (1 Peter 4:10–11)

How easy it is to drift or even become becalmed as a homegroup leader. God's plans for you are far better than that. His desire, for all of you, is not only to be blessed by the Holy Spirit but also use the gifts he has given you to be a blessing to everyone in your group. Edification and blessing are the marks of the work of the Holy Spirit.

1.7　In a nutshell

- Homegroups can play an important part of the life of the church, helping to provide fellowship, caring, teaching, and encouraging evangelism.

- All of us need the friendship and fellowship of other Christians.

- Witnessing needs to begin with people you already have a relationship with: family, friends, and neighbors.

- The Holy Spirit is the unseen leader of the group; you are just his co-leader.

- Encourage each other to identify spiritual gifts and encourage their use and development.

1.8   Recommended reading

How to Lead Small Groups by Neal F. McBride

Becoming a Contagious Christian by Bill Hybels and Mark Mittelberg

The Spirit-filled Small Group by Joel Comiskey

PART 2:

CARING FOR HOMEGROUPS

CHAPTER 2

KNOWING YOUR HOMEGROUP

2.1   We are all different

I was brought up in a loving family with parents who believed in God but did not consider church attendance necessary, although they did send me to Sunday school. Through the witness of my Sunday school teachers, Mom started to attend church and came to a personal faith in Christ. Dad remained true to his convictions; he had nothing against the church but it was not for him. It was twenty-five years later, when Dad was in his mid-sixties, that he committed his life to Christ.

I later had the privilege of Mom and Dad attending my homegroup. Dad enjoyed asking questions, while Mom was happy to listen. My parents were good people, whose lives and faith were uncomplicated. They had no desire to wrestle with theological doctrines; it was sufficient to know the love of Jesus. Homegroup provided them with a safe and secure place where they could be themselves and ask questions without fear or embarrassment. Sadly, Mom and Dad are no longer with us and are missed by the group; not for their eloquent prayers, in fact neither of them would pray aloud, but simply for who they were.

This was a special time in the life of our homegroup. God had brought together a diverse group of people who cared for and encouraged each other, including Jim. Jim always arrived for homegroup before anyone else, eager to share the events of his day. The doorbell would ring half-an-hour before homegroup was due to begin, and it would be Jim. He would ask if he was too early, I would reply that it was fine and ask him to come in. To be honest, it wasn't ideal, as we had set aside this time for those last minute tasks. We needed to finish the washing up, vacuum the living room, and put the children to bed. He was happy to pick up a tea towel and help with the washing up, graciously accepting we were unable to give him our full attention. Chatting with Jim was enjoyable, for he was an interesting person.

By the time the rest of the group arrived, Jim was no longer chatty. He had now become quiet and reserved. He found it difficult to participate in conversation with the rest of the group, even though he knew them all well. Despite my disappointment, I had to accept that Jim was more comfortable being a listener than a contributor.

These stories about Mom, Dad, and Jim are not unique. There are probably more people than we realize who have to overcome their inhibitions to take part in a homegroup. We cannot over-emphasize the importance of getting to know your group. We are not suggesting you should keep an exercise book to note down everyone's idiosyncrasies; but it is helpful to understand your group as individuals and show sensitivity towards them. How many people have left a homegroup hurt by insensitive comments or afraid of embarrassment, unable to share the real reason for no longer attending? There is a difference between knowing about a person and really knowing them. Take a few minutes to check out how well you know the people in your group, both personally and spiritually.

How well do you know your homegroup?

SPIRITUALLY

- Have they made a personal commitment?

- What is their level of biblical knowledge?

- Are they maturing as a Christian?

- Do they find the homegroup spiritually helpful?

- Are they willing to pray or read aloud?

PERSONALLY

- Are they comfortable sharing personal issues?

- Do they have any health or dietary problems?

- Are they at ease during homegroup?

- Do you know their family situation?

- Do they enjoy attending your homegroup?

What a difference it could make if you devoted a little more time getting to know the people in your homegroup. You cannot be expected to know everything about each person in your group so things may inadvertently be said that touch a raw nerve. However, a little extra awareness could go a long way to ensure everyone feels safe and secure.

2.2   Who is in your group?

Throughout our twenty-five years of leadership, we have appreciated the diversity of people with whom we have shared a homegroup. We consider the hallmark of a balanced group to be one that is able to accommodate a breadth of personalities. But sometimes there will be one person who tries to take over and the group cannot cope with this. For example, you may have a dominant person with strong opinions who believes it is his or her God-given right to claim the last word in every discussion. Alternatively, the problem could be an inactive member who uses the opportunity of the Bible study to catch up on sleep. Harmless as this may seem, it can have an unsettling effect upon the other members of the group. Both these examples are not necessarily serious in themselves, but if they begin to infringe upon the group, it will be necessary "to step up to the plate" and take some action.

There are three character types who are most likely to cause problems: the difficult people, the offensive people, and the passive people.

The difficult people

The dominant: *Tries to take control*

The last word: *Always has a final comment*

The small talker: *Boring!*

The single topic: *Brings all conversations back to their pet subject*

The self-opinionated: *Believes they have all the answers*

Often people are a mix of these—for instance, the dominant people want to take control, give all the answers, and make sure they have the last word, and they often have a pet issue which they will wax lyrical on for ages! The question is, how do you handle these people without falling into the trap of becoming like them? As the leader you must remain in control so that everyone understands that it is your decision to continue a conversation or draw it to a close. Achieving this will depend upon your own personality and style and can be done in several ways.

- When the person pauses for breath politely but firmly take back control, acknowledge their contribution, and invite others to share their views.

- If their habit is to interrupt when someone else is speaking, don't acknowledge them or make eye contact. Instead, look at the person who has been interrupted and confirm you wish them to carry on speaking.

However you handle the situation, it is important the person is left in no doubt that closure has taken place and she does not have a further platform to respond. This has to be done with sensitivity and without embarrassment, as you do not want to put the person down nor squash her willingness to contribute. It needs to be more a question of how much she contributes and when.

A useful tip is to take a lesson from the professionals. The next time you are listening to an interview on the TV or radio take note of how the interviewer always remains in control and draws the conversation to a close, as and when necessary. An interviewer who is a master of this is Oprah Winfrey. She is always polite but never leaves the guest in doubt that it is time to move on in the conversation.

The offensive people

The rude: *Makes the conversation personally offensive*

The socially inadequate: *Manners and hygiene not a priority!*

People in this category may not be aware that they are causing offense. It is extremely unpleasant to be with someone who has personal hygiene problems or who makes comments that are insensitive or just downright rude. These problems cannot be ignored and have to be addressed, or they may become a reason for people to leave the group. Difficult as it may be, your responsibility is to speak sensitively to the person in private, making him aware he has a problem and needs to do something about it. This, undoubtedly, will be a difficult conversation, and it is advisable to have discussed first what you plan to say with someone you respect for his or her wisdom.

And then what? It is easy in theory, difficult in practice! First, the person may not appreciate being spoken to regarding this issue and may not even agree that she does have a problem. Secondly, there is not always a quick fix solution. My advice is if you have been bold enough to tackle the situation, try to see it through to the end, hard as it may be.

The passive people

The sleeper: *Within five minutes they are in a world of their own*

The hard of hearing: *So much noise that they find it difficult to hear*

The listener: *Seldom takes part*

Usually, we take the view that if someone falls asleep in one of our meetings, he may not come away *blessed* but at least he will be *refreshed!* It can, however, be off-putting to the other group members if someone is apparently so uninterested she has fallen asleep. The reason why people doze off is more to do with the environment than lack of interest. For those who are experiencing difficulty with hearing, a little more thought to the seating arrangements, room temperature, and encouraging people to speak up could make all the difference. Eye contact and body language will help, as will speaking more slowly and clearly. Having key points written on a hand-out may also be helpful. (There may also be practical ways in which someone may need help, but this will depend on the individual's situation and should of course be treated very sensitively.) For the reluctant person, involving her in the conversation without causing her embarrassment may encourage her to take a more active part. Splitting people up into twos to discuss issues can mean that even if she won't share in front of the whole group, she will at least get to say something to someone!

Hang onto the reins

Every Saturday morning when I was ten years old I would be found in the local cinema watching classic Western movies, totally captivated. The sound of discharging rifles and galloping horses, mingled with the sight of the Wells Fargo stagecoach being pursued by outlaws, filled my imagination. The stagecoach chases kept me on the edge of my seat but in reality the life of a stagecoach driver would have been far more monotonous. They would have spent hours on end sitting on a wooden seat loosely holding the horses' reins. Only when the outlaws attacked would the stagecoach driver tighten his grip and take firmer control of his steeds. As leaders, you should be like the stagecoach driver, always in control but knowing exactly when to tighten your grip.

2.3   Encouraging one another

Ruth was in her early twenties, a psychiatric nurse-trainee, away from home for the first time and a regular member of our homegroup. It was not unusual for her to visit us after finishing an evening shift, pale and drawn, with tears in her eyes. She felt as though she had the weight of the world on her young shoulders; as far as she was concerned prayer and counseling were the only answer. We considered her immediate needs to be somewhat different, and would have listed them as having a hot meal, enjoying some encouraging conversation and, above all, getting a good night's sleep. Having provided all these, the next day the phone would ring and a bright and bubbly Ruth would say, "Thank you for your friendship and the meal last night. I feel so much better today."

We are not suggesting a cup of coffee and a chocolate cookie solves all problems, but there is always a danger of over-spiritualizing everything and assuming that all our needs can be answered by prayer. When Elijah ran away from Jezebel after his encounter with the prophets of Baal, the first things God provided for him were rest and food—not a pep talk. We need to be aware of people's practical needs as well as their spiritual needs. A word of encouragement or a birthday remembered can go a long way to meeting the needs of those in your homegroup. Just taking the time to write someone a note of thanks is always appreciated.

If it hadn't been for the phone call from Karen asking for a lift, I probably would have given homegroup a miss that night, as I was tired and struggling with a heavy cold. The evening didn't improve for me and the study notes did little to capture my imagination. How I longed for a hot mug of cocoa and my warm bed! The next morning, feeling slightly better, I opened up my computer to read the overnight e-mails. There was one from Carol, a member in the church who had attended another homegroup the previous night. It read:

> "Just to thank you for the Bible study notes; the text last
> night was particularly refreshing."

How interesting that Carol should send me a thank you e-mail about the same notes I had found tedious—despite the fact I had written them! All it took was a short e-mail of encouragement to cheer me up. Which of us does not respond positively to a word of encouragement? The simplest of remarks can lift our spirits. Why then are we so bad at encouraging one another? Do you find it embarrassing to pass on a compliment? Are you concerned that your words will be misunderstood or seen as patronizing? We all need encouragement to hang in there, to cope with the challenges of life.

Have you ever considered sending someone in your homegroup a letter of encouragement? We recently received one from Lillian which read:

> Dear Mandy & Steve,
>
> Thank you so much for having me last Sunday to lunch. Thank you for catering to my needs. I was completely relaxed with you. Your beautiful home has got such a lovely atmosphere of peace and joy. Thank you for being Jesus to me.

2.4   A life-changing encounter

The dawn chorus that morning was no different from any other as the Samaritan woman awoke. The cockerel crowed in the yard, children laughed, and the man she lived with still asleep in their bed. This was just the beginning of another ordinary day. The routine chores were followed by the long walk to fetch water from the well in the heat of the day. She had no idea that this was going to be an extraordinary day, nor that a brief encounter with a stranger, and a request for a drink of water were going to change her life.

Jesus and his disciples left Jerusalem and made their way north to Samaria, stopping at the village of Sychar. While the disciples went to the village for food Jesus rested at Jacob's Well.

The Samaritan woman arrived at midday to fill her water containers. The custom was for the women to draw water in the cool of the morning and evening, but this woman chose to come alone at the hottest part of the day. She wanted to avoid the other women because of the immoral life she led. Jesus took her by surprise when he asked for a drink. She was both a Samaritan and a woman of ill repute, and normally an upstanding Jewish man like Jesus would never have spoken to her. Jesus knew she needed acceptance rather than rejection, forgiveness instead of judgment. He did not use what he knew about the Samaritan woman publicly to embarrass or condemn her but instead shared the message of salvation.

Our lives and circumstances are vastly different from that of the Samaritan woman. Nevertheless, Jesus accepts us for who we are, despite our faults and failings. As homegroup leaders, you also need to get to know those whom God has entrusted to your care—their family and work situations, fears and dreams. Do you know their testimony or favorite worship song? Are you aware of any anxieties they may have over praying aloud or reading in public? Just as Jesus valued the Samaritan woman, so you should value every member of your homegroup.

The woman left her water jar beside the well and went back to the village and told everyone, "Come and meet the man who told me everything I ever did! Can this be the Messiah?" (John 4:28–30)

Many Samaritans from the village believed in Jesus because the woman had said, "He told me everything I ever did!" (John 4:39)

Just a thought

Our grandson, Charlie, was a cute baby until the age of nine months. Then overnight a toddler emerged with a mission to see the world. His big brown eyes were intent on hunting down new places to conquer as he crawled on all fours, yelling in baby talk, "Catch me if you can." His wise parents knew that even a toddler needs rules and boundaries, not to deny him freedom or new experiences but to provide safeguards and security. Just as parents need to be mindful of their children, leaders also need to stay in control and not allow the group to say, "Catch me if you can."

2.5 In a nutshell

- How well do you know the people in your homegroup? Remember there is a difference between knowing *about* a person and really *knowing* a person.

- Leaders should be like stagecoach drivers, always in control but knowing exactly when to tighten the reins.

- Just a little encouragement can go a long way.

- If Jesus accepts and loves us for who we are, we also should accept and love the people in our homegroup for who they are.

CHAPTER 3

CARING FOR YOUR HOMEGROUP

3.1   Caring is a privilege

It was the novelist Dorothy L. Sayers, writer of the Lord Peter Wimsey mysteries, who first penned the expression, "A trouble shared is a trouble halved." Which of us has not been grateful to family or friends for their care and support when experiencing tough times? Homegroups should also be a place where care and love abounds. Looking back over many years it has been our privilege to care for people while they have been part of our group. We can recall two such occasions.

The phone rang; it was June. "Hi, my son, Matthew is preparing for his Beaver Scout badge in computing and needs assessing. Are you free Tuesday evening to test him? Nothing difficult: he just has to prove he knows the basics." "Delighted to help," I replied. My response to June was warm and accommodating; but my thoughts were somewhat different. Tuesday really wasn't the most convenient evening, as I had set it aside to write this piece on caring. Admittedly, I had said all the right words but I resented giving up the time. However, true to my promise, I went to see Matthew on Tuesday evening. My intention was to spend a quick ten minutes testing him and then be on my way. I was amazed how quickly time passed; I had forgotten to take into consideration the infectious enthusiasm of a young boy eager to show off his computer skills. Looking back, I have no doubt who enjoyed the evening most: me. How easy it is to become so absorbed in your own priorities that you begrudge giving time to others. After all, the giving of ourselves is undeniably one of the most precious things we have to share.

On another occasion we received a telephone call from a member of our group asking if we could look after their three children as their mother had unexpectedly been taken into the hospital. Mark was ten, Sue was eight, and John was five. Including our own, we now had five children between the ages of three and ten. This was a logistical challenge: they were all at different schools, went to bed at different times, and I dare not mention their dietary requirements! But don't get this story out of perspective—what we did was nothing exceptional. This however, was not the opinion shared by the Watkins family who saw it simply as an answer to their prayers. They considered our support to be more than spiritual; it was practical, there when they needed it most. At the time we never fully appreciated the extent of their gratitude for what we had done. After all, caring for three additional children for a week and cooking a few extra meals didn't really disrupt our family routine that much. The Watkins family remains close friends and Mark still teases us about being permanently effected by having to eat cabbage!

We understand only too well the restraints that are on your spare time, which can stop you from caring for your homegroup in the way you would like. Make an effort not to allow your life to become so congested that you can only care for your homegroup by the occasional telephone call, asking, "How are you? It seems weeks since we last spoke." It is all too easy to allow the people you are meant to be caring for to become a nuisance rather than a blessing.

3.2   Pastoral care

It is impossible to split the topic of caring into neat categories; invariably most people and situations are too complex to fit into any one box. Having said that, we can place the story of Matthew and the Watkins family under the heading "practical help." There is another side of caring which we would define as "pastoral care." This is caring for people where they need more than just practical assistance. It usually involves the providing of emotional, spiritual, and practical support and can require long-term commitment on the part of the care-giver.

To illustrate what we mean by pastoral care, it may help to share a situation that happened in our homegroup some years ago. Sarah had offered to help friends look after their children while they spent the day packing in preparation for a house move. Before going back to her own home she put the children, including the baby, to bed. Later that evening we received a phone call telling us that the baby had died not long after being put to bed; a crib death. We were asked to break the sad news to Sarah and knew this was not going to be easy. We have no doubt that God, in his wisdom, granted us space in our busy lives over several months to support Sarah as she came to terms with what had happened.

As the homegroup leader, you will invariably have the main responsibility for the pastoral care of the group. Having said that, pastoral care need not necessarily be the exclusive responsibility of the leader; often there are others within the group who are both willing and able to provide support. However, discernment is required before involving other group members in pastoral care. You have a responsibility for the well-being of both the person who requires support and the person providing it. This is not a heavy-handed approach to leadership but simply applying common sense. We do not doubt, for one minute, that God uses individuals for his purpose in ways that amaze but equally he has granted us the gift of discernment, which cannot be ignored. It would be an over-generalization to state that everyone should be involved in pastoral care; nevertheless most people have a role to fulfill. Sometimes you just need to give more thought to what that role is!

It is essential to appreciate the difference between pastoral care and counseling and understand what pastoral care is not. It is not taking on the role of a therapist or counselor without the necessary professional training. You should acknowledge that it is unwise to give advice outside your scope of understanding, both spiritually and practically. It is not an admission of failure to recognize your limitations and that there are circumstances that are best dealt with by professionals. Your role in these situations is to be a friend and provide the support and encouragement that will invariably be required.

We apologize if it appears we have written more warnings than blessings about providing care. Please view them as good advice that will only enrich the way both you and your homegroup care for each other. Do not wait for problems or crises to touch your homegroup before you sit up and begin caring for them; it should be part and parcel of your everyday leadership.

3.3   There is more to caring than coping with problems!

We do not want to give the wrong impression, that providing care is about staggering from crisis to crisis. From our experience, the majority of people in the group have uncomplicated lives and will place few demands upon you. This is not to imply they do not require care but rather the type of care needed is more an appreciation of who they are. They all need to know that the homegroup values them. In other words, the little things you do are as important as the grand gestures. For instance, remembering to send everyone a birthday card or a get well soon card if they have been under the weather—these things matter. Have you ever thought about organizing a surprise party for a member who is celebrating something special? Trevor and Pippa, in our group, celebrated their Golden Wedding anniversary and thought they were just coming to dinner with us. To their surprise, the whole group was there to join in the occasion.

There may be some, who through no fault of their own, are unable to attend regularly, possibly because of work or family commitments. How about sending a note saying that the group misses them? It may not change the number of times they attend but at least they will feel valued. What about the person who would love to belong to a group but can't attend for practical reasons; a single parent who has to look after the children or an elderly person who is uneasy about going out at night? Why not take the homegroup to them? Or have you ever thought about doing some of the following:

- Offering to baby-sit

- Providing transportation for a hospital appointment

- Helping with the house and yard chores when someone is ill

- Visiting people, regardless of age

- Making a "we missed you" phone call

- Sending a bunch of flowers

Enjoy looking after your group. Believe me it is more fun than hardship! We understand finding the time can be difficult and that is why you will need to share the joy and the load.

3.4   More than glue

I make regular business trips to Eastbourne, leaving at 6:00 a.m. to avoid traffic congestion and invariably arrive early for my appointment. With time to spare, what should I do? Catch up on the paperwork, make a few phone calls, or visit a nearby home improvement superstore? You've guessed. I have become an expert in store browsing; even adhesives and glues now intrigue me. Do you know how many different types of glue there are? I've come across everything from super glue for invisibly mending that damaged family heirloom to the glue stick for the scrapbook. Different needs and applications require a different glue solution. I found these useful gluing tips on the internet:

- It is essential to use the right type of glue.

- Too much glue can create problems.

- Too little glue is always a problem.

- Apply the glue evenly.

Wandering around home improvement stores looking at the glue displays may not have been a totally worthless pursuit. Just as there are different types of glue, people also need different kinds of love and care, depending upon their situation. The circumstances may not always need a super glue solution, just a quick dab from a glue stick.

Perhaps glue and care are not so vastly different; both bond things together!

- It is essential to use the right type of care.

- Too much care can create problems.

- Too little care is always a problem.

- Apply the care evenly.

Can you imagine life without glue? How many toys and pieces of furniture would fall apart? Similarly, a world without care would fall apart. We all need it, can't survive without it, and have a responsibility to share it. Make sure your homegroup is bound together by the glue of care!

3.5 Guidelines for caring

Accept your limitations

There may be occasions you have to acknowledge, both to yourself and the person to whom you are providing care, that additional support and advice would be beneficial. Accept your limitations, both professionally and practically. (See 5.1 Spread the joy and the load.)

Listening is essential

An essential part of care is having the ability to be a good listener. Listening involves more than using our ears, it requires our full attention. It is all too easy to follow a conversation without understanding what the person is really trying to communicate. Patience is also required, as the person may not find it easy to express his feelings in words. Listening needs to be undertaken with a genuine respect for the other person, showing empathy for his situation. (See 5.3 Effective listening.)

Practice confidentiality

Confidentiality should not be taken lightly when caring for others. This is not necessarily because the matter at hand is of a sensitive nature but because people need to know you are not a gossip. If you really need to share the situation with someone else then ask permission of the person requiring help, explaining your reasons why. (See 5.2 Confidentiality.)

Be honest

Caring for people has its challenges, including having to speak honestly even if you know it is going to mean having a difficult conversation. Avoid coming across as superior or judgmental. Make sure any facts have been verified before bringing them into the conversation. Telling the truth, even in love, does not always get a warm reception.

Seek support

There can be real dangers in becoming over-involved while providing care and support, to the point that it begins to have an adverse effect upon you, emotionally and physically. It is advisable, in these situations, to have someone you can confide in for guidance and support.

Prayer is essential

You should never undervalue the importance of prayer when caring for people. Nothing should drive us to our knees quicker than the realization of the responsibility we have taken on when we became involved in other people's lives. Above all else, our caring should be a window through which our Lord Jesus Christ can be seen.

Just a thought

All of us like to tell stories of celebrities we have met. I recall my encounters with Maurice Gibbs from the BeeGees and astronaut, James Erwin. Are you impressed? Perhaps, I should be more honest. I just happened to be in a restaurant where Maurice Gibbs was dining, and as for James Erwin, we were attending the same convention. The word "encounter" now sounds somewhat stretched—I spoke to neither of them, nor did I catch their gaze. Being seen with celebrities can do wonders for our egos and story telling!

Wanting to sit next to the right person was no different two thousand years ago, as Jesus showed in his parables. Was it this that led the disciples to neglect the foot-washing custom before the Passover meal? When Jesus and the disciples arrived at the Upper Room, the preparations had already been made for the Passover meal. The disciples, in their eagerness to sit next to Jesus, ignored the custom of foot washing before the meal. None of the disciples seemed keen to adopt the role of the servant. Jesus, knowing their hearts, used this opportunity to wash their feet to teach that the qualities of a true leader are a willingness to undertake the tasks others consider beneath them. The disciples were ashamed, as they knew they should have washed their master's feet, not the other way around. We cannot think of a more vivid illustration of showing servant-like qualities than washing another person's feet. We all have our own opinions about our bodies, that perfect six pack stomach or oversized nose, but we doubt if many of us would claim to have attractive feet! How far are you prepared to bend down to care for others?

"So he got up from the table, took off his robe, wrapped a towel around his waist, and poured water into a basin. Then he began to wash the disciples' feet and to wipe them with the towel he had around him" (John 13:4–5).

3.6   In a nutshell

- Caring for the homegroup does not need to be your responsibility alone; encourage the group to care for one another.

- Caring for people can sometimes be challenging, however, it also can be rewarding.

- Do not get out of your depth, practically or spiritually, when caring for your group. It is not an admission of failure to ask for help.

- Caring is seeking to offer practical assistance, bringing healing and wholeness in the name of Jesus Christ.

3.7   Recommended reading

Building Self-Esteem by Sue Atkinson

CHAPTER 4

WELCOMING YOUR HOMEGROUP

4.1   Welcome to our home

Invariably, our first words of welcome as we greet people at our front door are "Mind the step!" This is followed by "Don't be embarrassed. Everyone trips and falls inside." We have an unforgiving doorstep that will trip you and send you sprawling into the hallway. What a great way to say, "Welcome to our home!" Exaggerated? Maybe, but please don't miss the point. The welcome begins at the front door.

Can we introduce you to friends of ours, John and Joyce, who practice the gift of hospitality? Even before the final dong from the doorbell chimes fades away, the door is opened and you are lovingly invited into their home. Gone are the concerns of the day to be replaced by "We're glad you came to homegroup tonight!" Our coats are taken and hung up in the coat closet before we make our way into the living room, where a variety of teas and coffees are promptly served, together with home-made cakes and cookies. We are sure John and Joyce do not consider that they do anything exceptional in their hospitality. They are just being themselves; kind and caring, making everyone feel welcome and at ease in their home. Perhaps it takes as little as a warm embrace and a smile that says, "We're glad you came tonight."

So how do we make people feel at home?

- Greet people as they arrive.

- Offer a choice of refreshments—teas, coffee, and cold drinks.

- Have a seat for everyone.

- Remind people where the restroom is.

- Make sure you speak to everyone.

- Make sure you say goodbye to everyone.

4.2   Where and when

Where

As the word "homegroup" suggests, the best place to hold a group meeting is in the home, where it is easier to create a relaxed atmosphere. Easy chairs and soft lights take a lot of beating. Alternatively, groups may choose to meet elsewhere, from the church hall to the local coffee shop. The venue will depend upon the needs of the group. For instance, a young moms/dads homegroup might choose to meet in the church building, particularly if there is a nursery available. Wherever you meet, make sure the ambience is right and it is the most appropriate venue for all members of the group.

It is a good idea to hold the homegroup in the same location every time. If this is not practical, keep the number of venues to the minimum and ensure everyone is advised well in advance of where the meetings will be held. If it is possible, hold the homegroup in the homes of those who may find it difficult to attend regularly, because of a disability or finding someone to baby-sit the children. Alternatively, can homegroup members baby-sit on a rotation or provide help with transportation?

When

Traditionally, homegroups meet on a midweek evening between eight and ten o'clock but increasingly the "when" factor is being built around the working and social demands of the people within the groups. Groups should be encouraged to meet on days and times that best suit their needs. If at all possible, groups should meet on a weekly basis. This helps to build friendship, trust, and continuity, which are essential for a healthy homegroup. However, it may be better to have a homegroup that meets every other week, if people are definitely going to make a commitment to attend, rather than holding it every week with only a few people showing up each time.

4.3   Welcoming new people

Visiting someone's house for the first time can be a daunting experience. The only information you have been given is the house number and name of the road. Now let's make the challenge even more interesting; it's a dark winter's night, there is poor street lighting, it's raining and you can't read any of the house numbers—what do you do? After you have driven up and down the road four or five times with your prayers becoming more audible, you finally park the car. Eventually you arrive at the house, fifteen minutes late and ring the doorbell. After an interminable wait, the door opens and you are greeted with a monotone, "Hello" followed by, "Did you have any problems finding us? Most people do because they can't find our door number." Sound familiar? Now let's put this into a homegroup context. New people have been assigned to your group. How should you ensure you minimize their anxiety in finding your home and make them feel welcome throughout the evening?

Before the meeting

- Write or phone in advance to confirm meeting day, time, and place.

- Give clear, precise directions to your home; landmarks are a great help, i.e. "We're across from the BP gas station."

- As a fun way to say "Welcome" tell them balloons will be hanging from the front door.

- Advise them where to park or even make sure there is a place directly outside.

- Advise them in advance what you will be studying and, if you are using printed material, make sure they have a copy before the meeting.

- Inform the other group members you have new people joining, their names, and any other helpful information. (For example, they are married with two teenagers.)

On arrival

- Make them feel welcome and show them that you are pleased they have come.

- Tell them, and I would also suggest show them, where the restroom is.

- Introduce them to the other members of the homegroup.

- Avoid in-jokes.

- Include them in conversations.

During the meeting

- Avoid having conversations that criticize the church. For someone attending the group for the first time and who is possibly new to your church, this is not the most edifying way to make her feel at home. First impressions tend to be lasting impressions.

- Don't presume he will want to take part. The most seasoned Christians attending a group for the first time may be slightly reluctant to contribute. How then might a new Christian feel if asked to read or pray at his first meeting?

- Don't ask personal or direct questions that may embarrass or cause offense. Even seemingly innocent questions such as, "Why have you moved to this area?" could make her feel uncomfortable. It is far better to ask open-ended questions that invite her to share what she wants.

After the meeting

- Encourage your group to include them in conversations at the end of the evening.

- Contact them during the week and say it was good they have joined the group and you look forward to seeing them again.

Just a thought

Most of us have a tale to tell of a situation or place where we felt uncomfortable or were embarrassed and had one of those "sweaty palm" moments. The event and place are usually etched deep into our memories, never to be forgotten. It is all too easy to overlook the needs of others; we should make sure our homegroups are places where people want to return to.

4.4   Good timekeeping

As far as possible practice good timekeeping, avoid the trap of having a "rolling start" homegroup and try to make it a habit to start at a set time. This encourages good stewardship that will help prevent the "straggler syndrome," where you are never quite sure if everyone has arrived and when to begin. Equally, it is good to have a regular finishing time. Anyone who needs to get away promptly will be able to do so. A helpful guideline is to practice the two-hour rule, from start to finish. Everything, from coffee and chat to the Bible study, should fit comfortably into two hours, with time to spare. If the meeting lasts longer, it may be a sign of poor time management rather than a night of fervent prayer! Good timekeeping encourages people to come; poor timekeeping can be a reason to stop attending.

Disadvantages of a long meeting

- Maybe a reason for people not attending.

- Mental and physical fatigue.

- Can be a poor use of time.

Disadvantages of a short meeting

- Meetings can be superficial.
- Friendships do not necessarily develop.

4.5   Are the children in bed and the dog locked up?

Our homes are, without question, the best places to host a home-group. There you can create a warm, relaxed, and peaceful environment, free from the everyday stresses of life, a place for meditation and prayer. . . . If only! But what about the children and dog? We should not assume everyone is at ease with children and pets, especially dogs. It may be everyday life in your family for the children to run amok at nine o'clock in the evening and the dog to become hysterical, but don't presume this is what everyone considers to be the ideal homegroup environment.

If you are not a dog-lover, it can be both an off-putting and frightening experience to open your eyes during the prayer time to come face to face with the bull mastiff. With its bad breath filling your nostrils, a glint in its eyes brings a new level of urgency to your prayers. Gone are all thoughts of world peace to be replaced by, "Lord, just grant me one small miracle: will someone please lock this animal in the kitchen!" And what about the hip homegroup leader, who calls time-out during the Bible study to change the baby on the living room floor and tries to make it acceptable by saying, "Carry on, just ignore us, sorry about the smell!"

I am not suggesting that children and pets should be locked away, never to be seen or heard, but rather sensitivity should be exercised, especially where pets are concerned. Not everyone is comfortable with animals and may even be allergic to them. An over-amorous dog or frightening animal can be a reason why people stop attending homegroup!

Just a thought

You might be surprised at the number of people who stop attending a homegroup because no one has bothered to tell them where the meetings are being held. So if it is necessary to hold the group in differing venues, everyone needs to know well in advance. This applies particularly to anyone who cannot attend homegroup regularly. The responsibility should not be on the member to contact the leader to find out the venue. A simple discipline for leaders is the where, when, and welcome principle. All it takes is a phone call to say where the group is meeting, confirming the time, and saying you are looking forward to seeing them.

4.6 In a nutshell

- A warm greeting at the front door, the children in bed, and the dog asleep all help to say, "It is good to see you."

- Attending a homegroup for the first time can be daunting. Make sure you turn it into a positive experience.

- Make sure everyone knows when and where the group will be held.

- Good timekeeping encourages people to come; poor timekeeping can be a reason to stop attending.

- If you have pets that roam the house, always make sure the people in your homegroup are comfortable with this. If they are not, you may be advised to put the pets in another room during the meeting.

CHAPTER 5

OVERSEEING YOUR HOMEGROUP

5.1   Spread the joy and the load

The quickest way to burn out as a leader is by falsely believing it is your responsibility, alone, to take on all the needs of the group, particularly practical requests. You are not a sponge with a limitless capacity to absorb. Unsurprisingly, there are some people who have a misconception of the role of a homegroup leader and see you as their "Jim will fix it." Inevitably, there are always a few individuals who have selective understanding of what is meant by reasonable and fair, and sometimes you will have to say, "Sorry, I can't help." You don't have to respond favorably to every request for help; each situation should be assessed as to whether it is reasonable and your responsibility.

On one occasion, I was leading a study from Acts 2 on how the early Christians helped and supported one another. I closed by saying if there was anything I could do to help anyone in the homegroup, they should not hesitate to ask. These seemed to be the appropriate words to say at the time but once spoken, I immediately forgot them. A few days later, Mary shared with me how much she had enjoyed the Bible study and asked whether I had really meant what I said about helping? Without taking a breath and before I could reply, she then asked if I could decorate her living room. Somewhat taken aback by her request I fumbled for a quick, stalling reply. "Mary, I need to think about it and get back to you." No, I didn't decorate Mary's room. In fact, I had to be honest and tell her I was unable to help on this. I felt bad about it but I had neither the time nor the necessary skills to carry out the work.

I learned some principles worth noting from this experience. First, if what has been asked is impossible or impractical, do not feel guilty about having to say you're sorry that you are unable to help. (This is something I am still trying to master!) Second, if the request is unreasonable, then you should not expect anyone else to take it on. Last, if what has been asked does warrant help but you can't give that help, there may be someone else in the group who can. I believe leaders have to share the load. As for Mary, a friend came to my rescue and decorated her living room.

5.2   Confidentiality

I was invited to attend a homegroup which was going to be discussing whether or not they should divide. They had a real logistical problem. Just how many people can you squeeze into a small room? I joined in the Bible study, sitting on the second step of the stairs, as there was literally no room in the living room. When the topic of dividing the group was raised, the conversation was fast and furious. No one disagreed with the idea in principle but the thought of change was not easy to accept. The tension was eased by a humorous comment, "Why would you want to split the group now? We have just reached the point where we can be rude to one another and still go home friends!" Reflecting upon the evening as I was driving home, I understood why there was a reluctance to divide. This was a caring group where trust had been established and sensitive topics could be discussed, with the knowledge that confidences would be respected.

Homegroups need to be places where all can feel secure enough to open up their lives to one another, without the concern that what has been shared will become gossip. It takes a great deal of courage and trust to share a personal and painful experience. How many people have stopped attending a homegroup because sensitive issues have been handled badly and confidences broken? If you are to encourage sharing, you have to take on the responsibility of keeping what has been said within the four walls of the homegroup, even if no formal request for confidentiality has been made.

At a homegroup I recently attended, one of the group shared that twenty years ago he had had a drinking problem. This was not to draw attention to himself but to help another member in the group put a similar problem into perspective. It was one of those silent moments as everyone listened to Dave, sharing from the heart his battle to overcome alcoholism. It was evident he was fighting to hold back the tears and was embarrassed by what he was saying. At no time did he ask that this should be kept in confidence but I believe all of us understood this was a private moment. What would be gained if we shared this story with someone else in the church? Would it help to build them up spiritually or would we simply be gossiping, betraying someone's unspoken trust in us to keep a confidence?

There are three types of confidentiality:

- An open secret.
- Shared in confidence.
- For your ears only.

An open secret

This is a personal matter that is openly shared within the home-group. Although there has been no request to keep it in confidence, there is nothing to be gained by passing the information on.

Shared in confidence

This is a personal matter that is openly shared within the home-group, on the understanding that it will be kept confidential. Trust takes a long time to build but can be destroyed in minutes by breaking a confidence through gossip.

For your ears only

This is a situation or problem that is shared only with you as a homegroup leader. Someone takes you into his confidence and requests guidance and prayer support.

It is possible that a confidence shared with you has ramifications beyond your responsibility or experience, yet the information cannot be ignored. My advice is as follows:

- Before promising to uphold the confidence, it is wise to explain that you cannot keep what she is about to share private if the confidence is about something illegal or involves harming herself or others (especially if it means a child could be at risk). Your church should have a child protection policy with which you are familiar.

- Do not get more deeply involved than your knowledge and ability on the issue allows.

- Avoid getting over-involved emotionally.

- Recommend he talk to someone who can deal with his problem professionally—either spiritually, medically, or legally.

- You should seek her approval before speaking to your church leader about what has been shared.

- Do not assume that what you are being told is the whole story; you may only be getting one side.

- You are there as a friend and homegroup leader; know your boundaries and how far you are willing to go to support him.

- Do not be judgmental.

Just a thought

We have all said things we regret, made loose remarks, or betrayed someone who trusted us to keep a confidence. How easily we slip into idle gossip that edifies no one! Who of us does not have etched in our memories conversations that we wish could be rewound and erased? One such occasion was when Mandy and I were in an Indian restaurant enjoying a meal with friends. We were deep in conversation about a young couple whose marriage had just broken up, when a diner from a nearby table came across and said, "That's my brother and his wife you are talking about." I cannot recall if we had said anything that was untrue, probably not, but that is not the issue. The fact is we were trivializing a situation that deeply affected his family. Regrettably, I probably still do enter into foolish conversation and gossip. However, that night in the Indian restaurant now serves as a constant reminder to put into practice the wise words of the apostle James,

> We all make many mistakes, but those who control their tongues can also control themselves in every other way.
> (James 3:2)

We do not believe there is a confidentiality scale. There is no category that carries the disclaimer, "I know I was told in confidence but I am sure they won't mind if I tell you." As Christians, it is important that we are true to our word. Never underestimate just how damaging unguarded words can be, either in conversations or when we publicly pray aloud. Perhaps something we should add to our To Do list as homegroup leaders is think before we speak.

5.3　Effective listening

Rarely does a week go by without Colin phoning me for a chat. He phones to bring me up to date with what has happened to him during the past week. This invariably turns out to be the same as the previous week. Why does he phone? Is there more behind his telephone call than just passing on his latest news? In a word, yes. Colin feels at ease sharing with me the everyday happenings of his life, not because I need to know, but rather because I listen to what he has to say with interest. Never overlook the significance of being willing to listen to someone. Anne Long, in the introduction to her book *Listening*,[1] says

It sounds simple and sometimes is, yet there is more to

1.　Anne Long, *Listening* (Darton, Longman and Todd: 1990)

listening than meets the eye. If some of the qualities needed in a good listener come naturally, others do not and need to be learned and worked at. Even the born listener can refine and improve his gift so that it becomes a deeper, richer ministry. For listening is a multi-dimensional activity. Hearing the words that someone speaks is to receive only one aspect of his communication. There are also other levels which need to be heard and understood—his style of speaking, his feelings, thinking, attitudes, body, silence. All these are dimensions of the person which we must learn to hear if we are to understand him.

There are probably many reasons why a person is a good listener or not. Are some people born better listeners than others? This is probably true, but it can also be true that we are too busy being busy to have time to listen. We can all improve our listening skills by putting into practice a few simple disciplines.

Listen to content not delivery

Not everyone has the gift of expressing himself or herself easily. Some may even be boring to listen to, or may have facial mannerisms that distract you. Remember to concentrate on the content of what is being said, rather than on the quality of delivery.

Maintain eye contact

Good listening is more than hearing the words; body language also plays a part. It is important to maintain good eye contact with the person speaking. It reaffirms that you are listening.

Avoid too much emotional involvement

Try not to become too emotionally involved as it will stop you being able to listen objectively and rationally. If what has been said causes you distress (and this is inevitable at times) you will need to have someone who you can turn to for support. (See 12.2 What is a homegroup pastor?)

Avoid distractions

Concentrate both on the person and what they are saying. Try to avoid becoming distracted by what is going on around you or by your own thoughts.

Don't interrupt

Ask questions to help with your understanding but don't try and take the conversation back. Remember you are doing the listening, not the talking.

Listen with sympathy

Try to sympathize with what the speaker is saying. It may not resonate with you but that should not stop you from listening with empathy.

Show respect

Not everyone is a sparkling conversationalist but everyone deserves to be listened to with respect.

Just a thought

Mike was the ideal person to lead the homegroup training. Perhaps being a policeman gave him an advantage in knowing how to teach listening skills. His presentation style was engaging, and it did not take long before everyone was relaxed and laughing as he used amusing illustrations to bring his points across. Nothing that he said was startlingly new to me: over the years; I have both attended and led seminars on listening skills. Nevertheless, what he said was a wake-up call for me to re-evaluate whether or not, in practice, I am a good listener. As a homegroup leader, you should not undervalue the importance of listening and we would encourage you to read up on how to be an effective listener. It is one thing to know about the techniques for effective listening but putting them into practice is altogether different.

5.4 Sharing

I regret that I had few meaningful conversations with my father. Sadly, he died several years ago. He was a quiet, unassuming, and private man who rarely expressed his true feelings. We would talk about the soccer results or how the slugs had attacked his cabbages, pretending that the issues affecting our family had never occurred. My father was from a culture and generation that kept their emotions private; the word "sharing" was not in their vocabulary. Sharing our thoughts and feelings with one another is probably something we do more naturally in today's society, although for many men the conversation still does not go beyond soccer, home improvement, and gardening. Sharing within the homegroup is a privilege, not a right. We should have the discernment to know when it is appropriate to encourage sharing; ensuring that what is being said is beneficial both for the group and the individual who is sharing. Sharing can be defined in the following ways:

- Common knowledge—the sharing of general information that everyone would appreciate or benefit from knowing. Example: "Mrs. Jones' funeral will take place at the church at 2:00 p.m. on Wednesday."

- Just the facts—the sharing of personal factual information that is not sensitive or embarrassing. Example: "Please pray for me as I am going into hospital for a minor knee operation."

- Personal—the sharing of the sort of intimate, personal feelings that are difficult to talk about. Example: "A few years ago I had an affair that nearly ended my marriage."

Useful guidelines for sharing

Lead from the front

Be prepared to take the lead. The amount of personal information you share will probably set the level within the group. Set boundaries so everyone understands what degree of sharing is acceptable.

Know when it is unwise to share

There are some things that may be unwise or unhelpful to share within the homegroup. Too much personal information may not be helpful to everyone in the group and some things are best shared one-on-one.

Don't run before you can walk

Usually people are reluctant to share personal issues until they feel secure. Encourage people to share at the common knowledge level, until they feel comfortable trusting the group with more personal information.

Be yourself

Sharing has to be normal, natural, and honest. We should not look to shock or embarrass each other.

Don't judge

Acknowledge what has been shared with love and acceptance, without being judgmental.

You don't have to share something!

Not everyone will feel at ease sharing. You should not make sharing a compulsory part of the homegroup.

Sharing is not gossiping

Make sure you are sharing and not gossiping. Gossiping is passing on information that you don't need to talk about and the other person doesn't need to know. Sharing is talking about issues that you both do need to know about.

Can I trust you?

To share personal and intimate details takes courage. Both leaders and homegroup members need to treat what has been said in confidence and respect the honesty and bravery of the person who has shared.

Just a thought

A few years ago, a TV commercial for British Telecom had as its slogan, "It's Good to Talk." Their intention may have been to encourage us to spend more time on the telephone for the benefit of their shareholders. Nevertheless, there is a truth behind the message—it is important that we talk to each other and have people we can confide in.

5.5   Dealing with criticism

Criticism will come in all shapes and sizes, from someone questioning what you are doing to comments on how you are handling a situation. You cannot escape or cocoon yourself from criticism, and at some time you will probably be affected by hurtful remarks, made to or about you. The question is, how do you handle them? Do you become angry, or do they make you want to give up? Don't be too hard on yourself. Don't set yourself impossibly high standards—you cannot meet the needs of all the people all of the time. Even with the best intentions, it is possible you will let someone down. You have to accept that some people's expectations of you are unrealistic. There will be those who never stop thanking you for all you do, even to a point of embarrassment. On the other hand there may be someone who has exactly the opposite opinion and is judgmental. This is more than hurtful; it also undermines your leadership.

How then should you deal with criticism? If you are non-confrontational, your immediate inclination will probably be to avoid speaking directly to the person in the hope the problem will just go away. This is not necessarily wrong, as the person may be going through a difficult period in her life and you just happen to be in the firing line. All she needs is some time and space. However, if the situation continues, it does need to be dealt with because her attitude may have an adverse affect upon the other members of the group. An attempt needs to be made to restore harmony. It will not be easy but it is necessary for you to speak with the person regarding your concerns, with the aim of resolving the problem. It may be the case that there is a misunderstanding that is causing the rift, and merely by talking one-on-one it can be rectified. If this does not sort the situation out it may be advisable for the person to move to an alternative homegroup. This may well be a positive move for everyone and should not be considered as a failure on your part. Unless you are made of rubber and everything bounces off you, even the mildest of criticism will hurt. Part of your responsibility as a leader is to know how to handle it. The following may prove helpful when dealing with criticism.

Listen

When you are criticized, possibly the hardest thing to do is to listen. Your natural reaction is to defend yourself. Try and listen and understand the other person's viewpoint.

Evaluate

Is there justification in what is being said? Are you confusing criticisms with helpful advice? It may be what has been shared is for your benefit. You should ask yourself if there is something positive you could do to improve or rectify the situation.

Share

There may be occasions when it is necessary to share what has been said with someone you trust and respect for his advice. This is not to seek an ally for your corner but to help you evaluate what has been said and to keep things in perspective.

Respond

If you acknowledge that the criticism is justified, it will require action to be taken on your part to improve the situation. Alternatively, you may have to confront the person who raised the criticism to explain why you feel their comments were unjustified.

Move on

Receiving criticism from time to time does not necessarily do any harm. It may even help to improve you as a leader and to keep your feet on the ground. You need to learn to handle criticism with maturity when it has been shared to build you up rather than knock you down, respecting those who have taken courage to speak out. When criticism has been shared unjustifiably, do not allow the anger or hurt to linger. We have all spoken words that we regret. The best advice, from my own experience, is to move on.

5.6   Highs and lows

How easy it is to become discouraged, feeling unappreciated and taken for granted. Do you ever doubt your ability or calling from God? Is now the right time to take a rest from running the homegroup? Are there occasions when you simply have to just hang in there, even if it feels like you are climbing a mountain, struggling to find a foothold, longing to reach the peak? Many of us will identify with the emotional highs and lows of leadership.

If we have painted a picture of homegroup leadership being 90 percent dangling from the end of a rope and only 10 percent being on top of the mountain, then we apologize; this couldn't be further from the truth. Imagine the exhilaration a mountaineer experiences on reaching the summit. Gone are the thoughts of giving up and turning back. For the majority of the time leadership is a pleasure but just like the mountaineer, we need to be well prepared for those challenging climbs. Don't forget God's calling on your life, and remember the Son shines at the top of the mountain. Hang in there!

> God has given each of us the ability to do certain things well. So if God has given you the ability to prophesy, speak out when you have faith that God is speaking through you. If your gift is that of serving others, serve them well. If you are a teacher, do a good job of teaching. If your gift is to encourage others, do it! If you have money, share it generously. If God has given you leadership ability, take the responsibility seriously. And if you have the gift for showing kindness to others, do it gladly. (Romans 12:6–8)

5.7 In a nutshell

- A good leader is one who knows when and how to spread the joy and the load. Do not be a sponge and soak up all the responsibility.

- Homegroups need to be a place where trust has been established and confidences respected.

- Being a good listener is as important as being an accomplished speaker.

- Sharing and gossiping are not the same. Make sure you are sharing and not gossiping.

- Handle criticism wisely, learn from it, and move on.

5.8   Recommended reading

Listening by Anne Long

CHAPTER 6

SOCIALIZING WITH YOUR HOMEGROUP

6.1　Time to relax

According to a recent health article, stress is currently recognized as one of the major causes of death throughout the world. The American Academy of Family Physicians reports that the majority of consultations with family doctors are for stress-related symptoms. Suffering from stress is not new—the respected American scholar and theologian, Henry Ward Beecher, who died in 1847 wrote, "It is not work that kills men; it is worry." Conversely, laughing has been clinically acknowledged to improve our general health and life expectancy. A little stress probably doesn't do us any harm; it may even be beneficial but it is important that we have an opportunity to relax and recharge our batteries.

Homegroups should be more than just a collection of people who regularly meet together for Bible study, prayer and the occasional meal and who say their goodbyes at the end of the meeting. Don't fall into the trap of relegating social activities into the category of when time permits. They are as important as any other aspect of a homegroup. Having fun together will help the group to gel and will nurture friendships that more naturally encourage care and support.

Jesus was not averse to spending time socializing and relaxing. He attended a wedding celebration with his mother and disciples that lasted for days (John 2:1–12). For Jesus, enjoying a glass of wine and laughing with friends was not a digression *from* his mission, it *was* his mission: being with people and sharing the good news of the kingdom of God.

6.2   Food, glorious food!

You don't need to be a Dickens buff to know who spoke the immortal words to Mr. Bumble, "Please sir, can I have some more?" The hungry Oliver Twist, goaded on by the other workhouse children, took courage and asked for more to eat. We may be a long way from a nineteenth century workhouse, but as the words of the song from the musical *Oliver!* remind us, food is glorious, and this is still a sentiment that is shared by most homegroups. If prayer, worship, and Bible study hold a group together spiritually, then it is calories that unite many groups socially. Food and homegroup go together like Laurel and Hardy, Batman and Robin, or more appropriately, apple pie and ice cream!

Take every opportunity to enjoy each other's friendship over a meal. This can be anything from a potluck supper to treating yourselves to an evening out at a local restaurant. It is also an opportunity to invite partners or friends of homegroup members who would not normally attend a Bible study. It is easier and less intimidating to engage in conversation while enjoying a gourmet salad or standing together watching the sausages burn on the grill. Be sensitive in what you do and say, particularly if invited guests are not Christians. Careless talk and over-zealous witnessing should not be on the menu.

A few suggestions for organizing a meal:

- Ensure you take into consideration all the dietary needs of the group, i.e. vegetarians or those who have food allergies.

- If a group member has special dietary requirements try and cater to their needs, rather than expecting them to bring their own food.

- When eating out, make sure the cost fits within everyone's budget.

- Always have soft drinks available. You do not want to encourage drinking and driving, and some people will prefer non-alcoholic drinks.

- If you have a potluck meal, don't get concerned if you have more snacks than desserts, or the other way round! Invariably there is more than enough to go around, plus leftovers.

- Don't leave the host to do all the preparation, clearing away, and washing up.

6.3   Out and about

Social activities are a good way to get to know the families of those in the group, including partners who do not normally attend, children, friends, and pets. Try to be inclusive in the activities organized. Don't arrange an event before discussing it with the group—not everyone may share your passion for bungee jumping!

What you do, when you do it, and how you do it will depend upon the mix of people in the group. Don't make your ideas over-complicated; a weekend away may sound great but requires a considerable amount of organization and has time and cost implications. An evening stroll along a river, followed by something to drink at a local coffee shop, generally gets the vote of approval from most people. Other suggestions you may wish to consider are:

- Weekend away

- Theater/cinema trip

- Country walk

- Bowling

- Games evening

- New Year's Eve party

- Barbecue/picnic

- Meal at a restaurant

- Potluck dinner

- Trivia night

Helpful guidelines when organizing social activities:

- Plan well in advance as schedules get congested.

- It doesn't have to be costly to be enjoyable.

- Arrange a variety of activities.

- Discuss ideas for social activities with the group before going ahead with any arrangements.

- Keep everyone informed as the arrangements unfold.

- When sending written invitations include partners even if they are not regular members of the group.

- Encourage single members of the group to bring a friend.

- Organize activities that include children if applicable.

- The simplest of social activities are often the best.

- Don't be disappointed if not everyone wants to attend.

- Encourage other members of the group to help organize social activities.

I am not suggesting spending a warm summer's evening with friends savoring the culinary delights of a grill will guarantee a stress-free existence. However, there are not only benefits for your own well-being in taking time out to relax and socialize, but you can also bring pleasure to others by simply spending quality time with them. Attending a homegroup should be a source of relaxation, not more stress and pressure.

6.4 In a nutshell

- You can bring pleasure to others by spending time with them.

- Jesus also relaxed and socialized.

- Enjoy each other's friendship.

- Social activities are an opportunity to get to know each other better.

PART 3:

TEACHING IN HOMEGROUPS

CHAPTER 7

LEADING THE BIBLE STUDY

7.1 A man of faith

I was saddened to hear that Dr. Kenneth Taylor, the author of *The Living Bible,* had died in June 2005 at the age of 88. As a teenager, I clearly recall lying on my bed reading a well-thumbed copy of *The Living Bible* with a renewed sense of understanding of God's word. My story is not unique; there are thousands around the world who owe a great deal to Dr. Taylor for paraphrasing the Bible into everyday language. I had no idea at the time that I would have the privilege of being a part of Dr. Taylor's worldwide ministry and eventually get to meet him.

Dr. Taylor grew up in a Christian family and from an early age read God's word but wrestled with the archaic language of the King James version. As a father, he was often disappointed that there were no books available that retold Bible stories for children. When his children brought home their Sunday school pictures, he wrote the Bible stories to match the pictures, using words and phrases they would understand. Originally Dr. Taylor had only intended the stories for his own family but they were eventually published in 1956 as *The Bible in Pictures for Little Eyes,* which is still a best-seller throughout the world.

Realizing there was a need for a greater understanding of God's word for adults, he began paraphrasing the whole Bible from the King James text. After several attempts the *Living Letters* was published. During the next few years, Dr. Taylor paraphrased the remainder of Scripture, and it was published as *The Living Bible.* His work was not complete, and in more recent years, he oversaw the publication of *The New Living Translation Bible.* My memory of Dr. Taylor is of a humble man who passionately wanted children and adults to read and understand God's word. His legacy will continue to touch the lives of generations to come. In Dr. Taylor's own words, "I learned that prayer brings power, but character grows through reading and obeying the Word of God—the Scriptures."

We undoubtedly live in privileged times with a proliferation of translations and paraphrases of the Bible, but I wonder if we are not a nation of Bible purchasers as opposed to Bible readers. Sadly, we are losing both the discipline and blessing of reading God's word. It is not the case that sharing in a Bible study is more important than worship or fellowship; they are all equally important. Do not allow spending time studying God's word together to be squeezed out. As a homegroup leader, take seriously the importance of Bible study for your group.

7.2 The role of the Bible study leader

The Bible study leader should be like the captain of a soccer team, tactically prepared, leading by example and more concerned about the team succeeding than being recognized with the award for "man of the match." Similarly, the Bible study leader should be well prepared, lead by example, and not dominate the discussion by wanting to be "man of the study." Your role is to be an enabler, to help lead the group to a deeper understanding of the word of God and how it applies to their lives. This will be achieved by:

Encouragement

- Try to involve everyone in the group.

- Look for opportunities to affirm the group members and make them feel valued. Everyone responds to encouragement, from the simplest appreciation of thanking someone for her contribution.

- Acknowledge everyone's participation.

Leading the study

- Keep the discussion relevant to the subject being studied.

- Be prepared to interject with insights or a good question when the discussion goes flat.

- Avoid spending too much time on one question.

- Accept more than one opinion or answer.

- Allow time for silence. Homegroups don't fall apart if every moment is not filled with talk; there are occasions when people just want to reflect quietly upon what has been said.

- Be flexible and willing to be open to the leading of the Holy Spirit, even if this means you don't complete the study.

- Watch the clock: it is not the length of the Bible study that signifies its success; it is more to do with the quality! Nothing is gained by burning the midnight oil.

- When something is said which is either factually or biblically incorrect, it cannot be ignored. Always give the speaker the benefit of the doubt and assume that he or she is trying to express something good rather than trying to lead the group into heresy. Seek clarification; he may just have chosen his words carelessly. But if there is an error, it will need to be corrected with sensitivity to avoid embarrassment.

Pitfalls to avoid

- Don't dominate—leading a Bible study is not about you. Your role is to facilitate so that others can share and learn.

- Don't embarrass people. This is easily avoided by not making assumptions. For instance, don't presume everyone is comfortable in taking part. Ask for volunteers rather than pressurizing someone.

- Don't make the studies judgmental; the aim is to encourage and build each other up spiritually, not to condemn.

- Don't go off on a tangent and avoid getting sidetracked with issues that do not add to the discussion.

- Don't ask personal or direct questions. Only ask those questions that allow for a non-embarrassing or non-personal response.

- Don't criticize your church, which can easily happen without people realizing it. There may be problems and issues that need resolving, but is the Bible study the right place for these discussions?

7.3   Who are you teaching?

It is important to know your homegroup so that you can lead a Bible study that is relevant to their circumstances and needs. For example, leading a study on witnessing in the workplace probably will not capture the group's interest if all the members are retired, whereas a study on "Does God value senior citizens?" would create a lively discussion. If the group you are leading is of mixed age and social interests, the same principles should apply. Choose topics to study that are relevant, regardless of age and background, such as "Witnessing to your neighbors." Make sure that what you are teaching is helpful and appropriate to those in the group, not just to you.

7.4   What study materials to use

Having decided on the most appropriate topic to study, the next question is should you research and write the notes yourself or look for material that has already been published? Not surprisingly, there is not a definite right or wrong answer as both options have advantages and disadvantages that need to be taken into consideration before making a decision. For example, it is worthwhile evaluating the cost involved in purchasing published material versus the time required to write quality study notes. Our advice is not to dismiss published material out right, we would recommend checking to see what is available before embarking on the writing of your own material. For many years we have written studies for homegroups, endeavoring to make the material relevant to the needs and spiritual seasons of the church. Perhaps it is the hours spent doing this that raises the question, "Has our time been well invested?" There is a wealth of published Bible study material available to meet the needs of all situations. We understand published study material may not completely meet the needs of your group and there is a cost implication, but we would encourage you to consider this option before embarking upon the task of writing your own material.

Another question is whether individual groups should make their own decision on what studies to do, or should there be a corporate theme that all the groups follow? On occasion, it may be appropriate to allow the church and individual homegroups to choose their study. Generally we would support a more corporate approach where all the groups follow the same theme. The advantage is that the studies will fit within the overall teaching program of the church. Although leaders like the idea of choosing their own topics there is always the danger that the studies never materialize, and the quality of the Bible studies goes down rather than improves. We all bring our own style and personalities to leading a study, so even if you are following a theme as a church, we have no doubt every group will have a slightly different flavor.

Writing versus buying

To help you with this decision here is some advice. Firstly, weigh the advantages and disadvantages of writing your own study versus buying material. Secondly, explore the multitude of published material already available. At the end of this chapter is a list of a few publishers who produce excellent Bible study materials for homegroups.

Writing your own material

ADVANTAGES

- Written specifically with the needs of your church or group in mind
- Saves money
- Follows teaching themes of church
- Pitched at the correct level between prayer, worship, and teaching for your church or group

DISADVANTAGES

- Requires someone to write material
- Requires printing and collating
- May be of uneven quality
- Huge writing commitment
- Requires theological accuracy

Purchasing study guides

ADVANTAGES

- No writing of notes required

- Material is proved and tested

- Wide choice available

- Different groups have the opportunity to study various topics at the same time

DISADVANTAGES

- Often offers too much material rather than too little

- Topics you wish to study may not be available

- Financial implications

- Too many studies on the same topic

Whatever decision you take, review the material being used regularly to ensure that it continues to meet the needs of your group or church. Even the best material, after a while, can become tedious or just boring. If you do decide to write your own material you will have to be able to accept criticism, as not everyone will like your presentation and style. Whether you are writing your own material or purchasing material, I recommend that you work out a two-year plan of study themes, with approximately four or five lessons on each topic.

Just a thought

My father's philosophy to do-it-yourself was straightforward—he never did it himself! He maintained it was quicker, easier, and more cost-effective to call in the professionals. The truth is he hated home improvement. When I look at my collection of tools hanging on the garage wall rusting away, I ask myself whether Dad had the right approach. A lesson my father's attitude taught me is to ensure that I have the skills and tools to do the job before embarking on any repairs. This philosophy is not only good practice for home improvement but is also helpful when it comes to leading a Bible study.

- Preparation is essential
- Use quality teaching materials

A poor workman blames his tools but even a skilled craftsman will find it difficult to do a good job with poor tools.

7.5   Preparing a Bible study

Devoting time to preparation is high on my list of priorities, not because I am a scholar but because I am the exact opposite. The only way I can lead a successful and enjoyable Bible study is by devoting sufficient time to preparation. It is not good to lead a study with no idea where you are heading.

In a recent interview with the BBC, quadruple gold medalist Steve Redgrave was asked about preparing for a race and this is what he had to say.

> Before the Olympics I would have two or three sessions a day. I would get down to the rowing club for 7:30 a.m. and start with about an hour and a half of endurance work on the water. The second session would be muscular so I'd spend some time on the weights. The third session would again be endurance, either on the water or in the gym. When we were on our intensive program, the number of sessions a day rose to four and a couple of times a week we would even add a fifth![1]

---

1.   BBC Sport Rowing and Water Sports Steve Redgrave answers your questions. www.news.bbc.co.uk/sport1/hi/olympics2000/rowing-andwater-sports/649763.stm.

Redgrave is acknowledged as one of the world's greatest athletes. I wonder where the line is drawn between God-given talent and sheer preparation and training. I suspect he would probably say somewhere around 30 percent gifted and 70 percent hard work.

For me, preparation means spending time alone prayerfully referring to Bible commentaries and searching for nuggets of insight that will enhance the study. You may prefer to use computer Bible software, while listening to your favorite CD. We are all different. The choice is yours but either way, there are a few principles that it would be wise to adopt:

- Do not skimp on your preparation.
- Read various translations of the passage of Scripture to be studied.
- If you are using written material, read it carefully several times so that you understand the aim of the study.
- Have the answers ready in advance to avoid having to think on your feet during the meeting.
- Refer to Bible commentaries and other resource materials for interesting facts and insights (See 7.11 Resource materials.)
- Spend time in prayer.

Just a thought

If I was asked to give one piece of advice at a marriage seminar on how to build a happy and lasting relationship, it would be this: always log onto a route-finding website to obtain directions before setting off on an unfamiliar car journey. This site gives step-by-step directions from your driveway to your final destination. Imagine how many arguments could be avoided between husband and wife as they slowly circle the same roundabout for the tenth time, disagreeing over which exit to take. Do your homegroup Bible studies also sometimes go around in circles with no apparent destination? If the answer is yes, this may be because there is a lack of thought about what should be achieved by the Bible study and how. Don't think of preparation as something you have to do; rather it should be something you *want* to do. The more you perspire before the meeting, the less you perspire during the meeting. To avoid a red face, sweaty palms, and embarrassment as you fumble through the Bible study, preparation is essential.

7.6   Constructing a Bible study

If you are choosing to produce your own teaching materials, there are a few basic principles that are worth bearing in mind and the most important is "Keep it simple." Over-complicated material with cryptic questions will not lead to a deep and meaningful study and will probably result in everyone feeling confused. One of the simplest Bible study techniques is to take a passage of Scripture and to ask the following three questions:

1.   What does the Bible say?

2.   What does the Bible mean?

3.   How does it apply to me?

Providing the passage chosen lends itself to this style of question, this is an effective method of Bible study.

An alternative method of constructing a Bible study is to use the Approach, Explore, Discover, and Apply technique:

- Approach: introduce the subject

- Explore: understand the meaning

- Discover: instructions and promises

- Apply: how does this apply to my life?

This is an easy-to-understand structure with a logical progression from an entry point of engaging interest to a personal application. To illustrate this method, let's look at the Bible story of the wise and foolish builders, as recorded in Matthew's Gospel (Matthew 7:24–27).

Approach

To engage your listeners' interest, talk together about how you have been affected by the pictures on your television screens of floods, storms, and hurricanes and their devastating effect on people's lives. This is an ice-breaking session and should not go on for too long.

Explore

Read the Bible passage to understand what Jesus is teaching. Using different translations and paraphrases will help the group in their understanding. You may also want to retell the story in your own words.

Discover

Look at the passage for instructions and promises. Questions that could be asked include:

- What are the consequences of only being concerned about the here and now?

- What responsibilities do you have to help non-believers consider the direction of their lives?

- What does it mean to build your house upon the sand?

- Having become a Christian, does that mean you are automatically building your house on rock?

Apply

Understanding without application is not enough. Each individual within the group needs to be able to go away and act upon the teaching. Consider the following questions:

1. Jesus should be the "rock" that we build our lives upon but how well do we know him?

2. Do you take time daily to read your Bible and pray?

3. What practical steps can you take to improve these aspects of your Christian life?

4. How do you make Jesus the rock on which you build your working life, your marriage, your relationships with others?

5. How does this affect the way you live, the way you spend your money, the way you vote?

All of us can benefit from improving our skills and techniques, no matter how long we have been leading a group. Nevertheless, it is all in vain if we do not have the desire for God's Word to touch our lives and those within our group. A verse in Matthew's Gospel puts it far better than we ever could:

> If one blind person guides another, they will both fall into a ditch. (Matthew 15:14)

7.7   Writing and asking questions

An important and challenging aspect of preparing for a small group discussion is the putting together of clear and easy to understand questions. If an explanation of a question has to be given, the question is probably wrong in the first place. This is possibly not because you have used too few words to explain what you mean; it is more than likely the exact opposite.

Good questions should:

- Be brief and understandable.

- Require more than a yes or no answer.

- Be unambiguous.

- Prompt a variety of valid and useful answers.

- Be relevant to what is being studied.

Below is an example that shows the difference between a well-constructed question and a poor one.

A poorly constructed question:

Do we have a responsibility to help people think about their lives and the direction they are heading, especially when it comes to ignoring the message of Christ?

A well-constructed question:

How can we effectively witness to non-Christians?

Having written a question, it is a good principle to test it on a family member or a friend. If your friend struggles to understand its meaning and finds it difficult to answer, we would suggest reworking it. The key to formulating good questions is clarity and simplicity.

Finally, a useful tip is to check that any questions referring to a Bible passage can be answered from various translations. Avoid the mistake of writing a question with an answer that can only be found in one translation!

7.8   Training is essential

Training should be a priority, both for individual homegroup leaders and to those overseeing this ministry within the church. I often speak to leaders, who enthusiastically want to talk about the caring and social side of their group, only to become embarrassed as they share the problems they experience in leading the Bible study. I am never entirely sure what response they expect. Should my reply be, "Don't worry, good fellowship is more important than Bible study?" Or do I say what I am really thinking, "Sounds like another case of not enough training!" I would urge those of you who have the responsibility of caring for and appointing leaders that more attention is given to the importance of training. It is unfair to expect anyone to take on a task for which he or she is poorly prepared. As in all aspects of training, it needs to be ongoing and not viewed as a one-time occurance. (See 12.4 Leadership training.)

7.9   It is worth the extra effort

It was a memorable day seeing my two-year-old grandson waddling up our front path, wearing his oversized coat and a broad smile. Charlie hasn't yet mastered the word "Granddad" so I have to be content with "Hi yer," which is his all-encompassing greeting to everyone from the mailman to the cat.

With a little help from his Mom, Charlie slips out of his coat and runs into his favorite room in our house, the kitchen. It is not because he is a budding Jamie Oliver; simply it's the easiest place for him to play with his toys on the smooth floor. It isn't long before I join him, pushing a toy car and attempting to make the sound of a Formula One racing car. My "vroom, vroom" noises probably only confuse him as he wonders, "Aren't I supposed to be the child around here?"

I suspect in years to come Charlie will not recall this occasion, whereas for me it has been etched into my memory under the heading, "treasured moments." Is leading a Bible study so vastly different from the joy I experience playing with Charlie? To savor this moment with my grandson requires me to give something of myself, both in time and a willingness to get on my knees and see the world through his eyes.

To enjoy, and we mean enjoy, leading a Bible study there has to be a desire within us "to get on the floor," and share in the privilege of exploring God's word together. I have no doubt if we all prayerfully put additional effort into leading a Bible study, we will encounter new blessings from God's word.

There is one bonus from playing with my grandson that I don't get out of leading a Bible study though: Charlie gives me a big kiss and hug before going home!

7.10 In a nutshell

- The role of the Bible study leader is to enable the group to understand and apply God's word to their lives.

- Make sure the topics you study are relevant to the group.

- Preparation should not be considered something you have to do; rather it should be something you want to do.

- We can all benefit from improving our skills and techniques, no matter how long we have been leading a Bible study.

- Training needs to be on-going and not viewed as just a one-time event.

- A homegroup without a Bible study is like a meatloaf without meat!

7.11 **Resource materials**

Journey through the Bible by Gilbert Beers

New International Bible Commentary by F. F. Bruce

New Bible Commentary by D. Carson, R. France, A. Motyer, G. Wenham (eds.)

Life Application Study Bible NLT

CHAPTER 8

LEADING WORSHIP

8.1   What is worship?

The topic of worship is one of the most contentious and fervently debated issues in church life. Should we only be singing the latest songs or raising the rafters with the hymns that have stood the test of time? Do we cast our vote of approval when we hear the beat of the drum or inwardly groan when the chords are struck on the church organ?

I recently attended a Grace Baptist Church whose members use the Evangelical Movement of Wales Hymn book. I suspect "Shine Jesus Shine" by Graham Kendrick was not number one on their song list.

As we sang the first hymn, accompanied by the organ, I was moved by the words we were singing: "To God be the glory! Great things He has done!" The hymn was written by Fanny Crosby in 1875 and was almost immediately forgotten until 1954 when it was used at the Billy Graham crusade in Harringay, London and became a firm favorite.

> To God be the glory! Great things He has done! So loved He the world that He gave us His Son;
>
> Who yielded His life an atonement for sin, And opened the life gate that all may go in.
>
> Praise the Lord! Praise the Lord! Let the earth hear His voice! Praise the Lord! Praise the Lord! Let the people rejoice!
>
> 0 come to the Father, through Jesus the Son: And give Him the glory! Great things He hath done!

In contrast, I was able to share in a service at the Brooklyn Tabernacle Church in New York, where Jim Cymbala, the author of *Fresh Winds, Fresh Fire,* is the pastor. A two hundred-strong choir, whose energy and exuberance filled the church, led the worship, and soon the whole congregation was on their feet, moving with the music and praising God with their voices. Although I was a stranger in this congregation of three thousand, I felt at home sharing in the worship. Throughout church history, music and singing have shaped our understanding of worship to such an extent we can sometimes forget worship is more than a song.

The story of how songwriter and worship leader, Matt Redman came to write the song, "Heart of Worship" is told in *The Purpose Driven Life*[1] by Rick Warren and may help us understand the true meaning of worship. "Matt Redman tells how his pastor taught his church the real meaning of worship. To show that worship is more than music,

---

1.   Rick Warren, *The Purpose Driven Life* (Zondervan, 2003).

he banned all singing in their services for a period of time while they learned to worship in other ways. By the end of that time Matt Redman had written the classic song, 'Heart of Worship.'"

> I'll bring You more than a song,
> For a song in itself
> Is not what You have required.
> You search much deeper within
> Through the way things appear.
> You're looking into my heart.[2]

The Bible has a rich tapestry of references to worship, from singing, to playing musical instruments, to dancing, to making a joyful noise. Moses rejoiced in praise after the Exodus, the Lord Jesus sang a hymn with his disciples at the Last Supper, and Paul and Silas praised God and sang hymns while in prison. Worship should be from the heart, whether it is singing or silence.

> Come, let us sing to the LORD!
> Let us give a joyous shout to the rock of our salvation!
> Let us come before him with thanksgiving.
> Let us sing his psalms of praise.
> For the LORD is a great God, the great King above all gods.
> (Psalms 95:1–3)

Our worship cannot be confined to our organized church services or homegroups; it has to be in every part of our life. Worship means submitting our lives to Christ; something that, if you are honest, you cannot do by yourself. You soon discover your human nature wants you to be self-centered rather than God-centered. God is aware of our human weaknesses and has therefore given us the Holy Spirit to be our encourager.

---

2.   Admin. by EMI Christian Music Publishing.

8.2 Worship in the homegroup

Worship in most homegroups is like a coal fire which is almost about to go out, lifeless with a few embers around the edges trying desperately to glow. In the extreme, sometimes this coal fire has never been lit! Let's be honest, do your group worship times really sparkle? In our experience they don't. This is not because of a lack of desire to spend time worshipping God but rather because leaders struggle to know how to lead worship in small groups. You are trying to replicate the worship from your church fellowship meetings, and it just doesn't work.

If you are to have a successful and rewarding time of worship there are four basic principles:

- Accept that you are only a small group of people and there is nowhere to hide.

- The time spent in worship needs to be appropriate to the group.

- Worship needs to be more than singing.

- Develop a desire to worship.

We have no doubt worshipping together in a small group could be far more rewarding if time was spent preparing and giving more attention to making the worship relevant to the people in the group.

8.3 Organizing worship

One of the reasons why worship in homegroups can sometimes be unfulfilling is because insufficient attention is given to the importance of organizing the worship in advance. If the same amount of time was devoted to organizing the worship as is given to planning the next social evening, we have no doubt our worship would reach new heights. True worship cannot be contrived, as it has to be an outward expression of our heartfelt love of God. Nevertheless, ten or fifteen minutes spent prayerfully preparing the worship would be a real benefit to your group.

Part of the problem is that many of us are people of routine; arriving at homegroup at the same time each week, always asking for the same drink and having the same conversations, "Have you had a good week?" Unintentionally our worship can take on the same uniformity, which is comfortable though not necessarily uplifting. Be encouraged: the solution is well within our grasp. All it requires is a little more attention given to organization and a touch of variety in how you worship together in homegroups.

To try to avoid worship becoming routine and familiar, why not regularly introduce new ways to express it? Invite people to choose a verse of Scripture to read, one which for them exalts the majesty of God. If you have a literary group, ask them to write a poem. If you are planning to do this, let the group know in advance so they can come prepared; no one likes to be embarrassed by being put on the spot!

Often we arrive at homegroup still rocking and rolling from the busy events of the day: work, children, and the dog. Consequently, we're not really ready to worship. We gulp quick mouthfuls of coffee, our minds still buzzing as we sing the first worship song; we've no time to take a breath. Does this sound familiar? Why don't you begin your worship with a time of silence and meditation? This will help the group to relax and clear their minds of the day's events and give them the chance to think about who they are worshipping. Imagine the difference it could make if more attention was given to organizing worship for the group.

> Sing praises to God, our strength. Sing to the God of Israel. Sing! Beat the tambourine. Play the sweet lyre and the harp. Sound the trumpet for a sacred feast when the moon is new, when the moon is full. (Psalms 81:1–3)

8.4   How to worship

As we have said, worship needs to be an outward expression of our love for God; therefore the style should be suitable and appropriate for the people within the group. The how will depend on who is in the homegroup. If the group has a member with musical gifts, then you are blessed with talent that will enable you to worship through music and singing. On the other hand, if your group has no one gifted in that way, there is no reason not to sing, even if the quality is somewhat suspect. Although worship has become synonymous with singing, a homegroup that doesn't sing at all is in no way missing out. It can be a real opportunity to be creative in alternative ways to worship. Avoid becoming routine worshippers, doing the same things week in, week out. Be imaginative and keep the worship both refreshing and meaningful by using a variety of different forms of worship. These could include:

Meditation

Silently meditate on who God is. It is a good idea to have a specific theme, for example, the wonders of God's creation. Before beginning a time of meditation, show a short clip from a wildlife or nature DVD or video that will help to focus the group's thoughts.

Read a portion of Scripture

Read portions of Scripture that express the majesty of God. The Psalms are a good place to start. For instance, Psalm 96 begins:

> Sing a new song to the LORD!
> Let the whole earth sing to the LORD!
> Sing to the LORD; bless his name.
> Each day proclaim the good news that he saves.
> (Psalms 96:1–2)

Prayers of praise and worship

Encourage the group to express their love and worship of God with short prayers acknowledging His majesty and glory. Share together a few suggestions before beginning; it will help the prayers to flow.

Celebrate communion

Paul, in his letter to the Corinthian church, tells them how they should conduct themselves before taking communion (1 Corinthians 11:17–34). His words are as relevant to us today as they were then.

- Acknowledge that Christ died for our sins. (v 26)

- Be reverent and respectful. (v 27)

- Examine yourself for any unconfessed sins. (v 28)

- Be considerate to others. (v 33)

A word of testimony

Invite people to share a word of testimony on what the Lord has been doing in their lives. These don't need to be long or even spectacular, just honest.

Read a poem

Not everyone feels at ease sharing a word of testimony or praying aloud but they may be more than willing to read a poem or a piece from a book that has touched their life.

Singing

Praise, rejoice, and honor God in your singing whether unaccompanied, singing along to a CD, or with the support of musical instruments. God listens to our hearts, not the notes we reach.

Listen to a piece of music

Listen to a piece of music that will help you meditate on who God is and his majesty. The choice of music may vary from a worship song to traditional hymns or a piece of classical music.

8.5 In a nutshell

- Worship is more than singing.
- It can be difficult to replicate the style of worship used in church to a homegroup meeting.
- Give attention to organizing worship in the homegroup. It will not always be spontaneous.
- Don't be afraid of silence in worship.
- Be creative.

8.6 Recommended reading

True Worship by Vaughan Roberts

The Purpose Driven Life by Rick Warren

The Unquenchable Worshipper by Matt Redman

CHAPTER 9

LEADING PRAYER

9.1   Understanding prayer in homegroups

Who of us would disagree that prayer is an essential part of the life of homegroups? If this is true, why do some homegroups consider their prayer life to be uninspiring, almost to a point of being forced? While many belong to groups that have rich and fulfilling prayer ministries, this is not the universal picture, and many groups struggle in this area.

I used to consider it was sufficient just to share a few prayer points before praying, to allow one or two people to pray and then wait for that prolonged silence which was the signal to close the meeting. Although this was not necessarily wrong, it was an indication of my lack of understanding of how the dynamics of a small group and prayer work together. I had failed to take into consideration two important facts. First, I wrongly assumed everyone knew how to pray and second, there is a difference between praying alone and praying in a small group. These are two important statements that need to be understood if the prayer life of your group is to be enriched.

Fledgling prayer

What do I mean by "fledgling prayer"? While sitting in the waiting room of my doctor's office, I picked up a magazine and came across an article about how young birds learn to fly, which intrigued me. I had naively believed birds were proficient in flight the first time they left the nest; apparently they are not. Birds are no different from young children learning to walk; it takes a combination of instinct and practice. The bird will begin with a routine of pre-flight checks, stretching and flapping its wings in the safety of the nest. The maiden flight then follows and invariably ends up as a crash-landing only feet away from the nest. Soon the short flights become longer, as the fledgling learns to use the wind for lift. Just as young birds master the art of flight, Christians (and particularly new believers) have to learn how to pray. Even the disciples, who spent all their time with Jesus, still had to ask, "Lord, teach us to pray." Therefore, it is not surprising that prayer in homegroups sometimes never takes off—we are still in the nest doing pre-flight checks. If I had stopped to think, it would have been obvious that fledgling birds do not have their pilot's license on their first flight. Equally, why would I assume everyone in the homegroup knew how to pray, particularly in a small group environment?

Formation flight

It is easy to assume that the reason prayer in the homegroup remains at the nest level is because the members of the group are not used to praying. In fact, it could be the exact opposite. The group may consist of people who are proficient in individual prayer but fail to understand there is a difference between praying on one's own and praying in a small group. They may even become frustrated that they are unable to pray as freely in the group as they do privately. Prayer in small groups is different from when we pray on our own: we have to learn to accommodate one another by listening and affirming each other's prayers.

Just a thought

You should never forget that it will be difficult, if not impossible, to lead the group into a deeper spirit of prayer than that which you have experienced yourself. The challenge for you as the homegroup leader is to make the prayer time a meaningful experience for everyone in the group.

- Praying does not necessarily come easily to everyone.

- Praying in a small group is different from praying alone.

- Praying together in a small group is as much about the other person's needs as your own.

I also tell you this: If two of you agree down here on earth concerning anything you ask, my Father in heaven will do it for you. For where two or three gather together because they are mine, I am there among them.
(Matthew 18:19–20)

9.2 Organizing prayer

To be honest, we have a slight hesitancy in using words such as "organizing" or "techniques" when referring to prayer. There is part of me that believes that gathering together and letting prayer happen spontaneously should be sufficient. Jesus teaches in Matthew's Gospel that where two or more believers pray in line with God's will their request will be answered (Matthew 18:19–20). When praying in a group of two or three, there is less need to adopt techniques. On the other hand, the more people who are involved, with their different levels of prayer experiences, the more the use of techniques can be beneficial. This is not to shackle prayer in the homegroup but to enable everyone to enter into a more fulfilling prayer experience. All you are doing is introducing ways that will help the group be more focused on what they are praying for. Before introducing new ways to pray, make sure everyone is comfortable with the idea. Don't produce it like a rabbit from a hat; share your plan several weeks beforehand to ensure the group is happy with it.

None of the ideas below are revolutionary, but they will help enable everyone to be more involved and focused on what you are praying for:

National or world issues

The television is a useful source of information. Record a news piece on a current national or world event, which should be no longer than two to three minutes. There should be no need to make any additional comments; the images and television commentary should be sufficient. After watching the news clips, ask the homegroup to pray about what they have seen.

Local issues

Go through your local newspaper and find an interesting and relevant article that affects the community. Avoid getting into a discussion over the article; the objective is to pray about the issue.

Church life

Pray for a different ministry within the life of your church each time you meet, everything from the Sunday school to the senior citizens group. To enable you to pray intelligently, you do need information about the groups, their leaders, and who attends.

Written prayers

Encourage everyone in the homegroup to write a prayer in advance of the meeting, which can be read aloud. Prayers don't need to be long; often the shortest are the most profound. Make sure everyone is comfortable with this idea.

Mission organizations

Adopt a person from your church or someone you know who is working for a mission or church organization. He or she could be working overseas or with a care agency in this country. Involve him in what you are doing as this is a two-way process, and he needs to stay in contact with the homegroup by letter or e-mail. If practical, encourage him to attend your group when he is in town or arrange a conference call. Make sure he feels part of your group and that he is aware of your prayers.

Homegroup members

Pray for each other within the homegroup; any personal issues that people are willing to share, families, and workplace situations. One way to do this is to pray for the person sitting next to you, as this ensures no one is left out.

Prayer journal

It is all too easy to pray and move onto the next hot topic. Why not keep a prayer journal and note what you have prayed for, from world issues to the lives of the people in the group. It is good to look back and praise God for answered prayer.

Ways to pray

Introduce different methods of praying into your group. They will help to keep the prayer time fresh.

- Twos or threes—divide into small groups for prayer.

- Silent prayers—don't be frightened by periods of silence. Allow time for people to speak to God.

- Pray for the person next to you; this is something you may wish to do in silence.

These suggestions are neither definitive nor exhaustive. There are many other ways to bring creativity into the prayer life of your group. For example, we haven't considered whether you should be seated, standing, or kneeling when praying.

Prayer co-coordinator

Few ideas are new. The problem is not the idea but how to find the time to implement it. Prayer is an important part of the homegroup ministry and warrants more time and effort than you are sometimes able to give to it as leaders. Where possible, ask someone else to take on the responsibility and privilege of leading the prayer time—perhaps giving her a grand title such as prayer coordinator.

9.3   Praying aloud

I would describe myself as a confident person when leading or speaking at meetings apart from one aspect—reading aloud. If ever asked to read aloud, having not previously practiced, I turn into a complete wreck from sweaty hands to sheer panic.

So what is your panic button—leading the Bible study, parking the car, or praying aloud in a meeting? All of us probably have at least one "Get me out of here!" area in our lives.

Possibly not everyone in your homegroup will feel at ease praying aloud. This may have nothing to do with their spirituality or your leadership; it is simply that they prefer not to pray in a group situation.

- It is important you respect each other's strengths, weaknesses and spiritual gifts.

- Don't embarrass or pressurize anyone.

- Reassure the group that it is great if they want to pray aloud and equally; if they don't, that's fine.

- Ask for volunteers to pray.

- Don't presume everyone has the same gifts as you.

9.4   Prayer is not gossip

Who of us does not get a buzz or boosted ego by knowing something which is not general knowledge? You should not confuse sharing items for prayer with gossiping. Perhaps it isn't too serious if you do inadvertently say something about someone's health but still a confidence has been broken. It is a habit you should guard against, for you may find yourself gossiping in your prayers about people and mentioning things in their personal lives that should remain private.

9.5   Prayer chain

It is good to develop the prayer life of your group beyond the meeting. If a need arises that requires immediate prayer, have a system in place by which everyone can be contacted. This may be done via phone or e-mail. The easiest way to do this is by setting up a prayer chain. The matter for prayer needs to go to the homegroup leader or prayer coordinator, who in turn will phone or e-mail the next member of the group on the chain and so on. Phoning is quicker! Be careful: messages can unintentionally become exaggerated or embellished. If there is one point below that is worth emphasizing, it is the need to write down the prayer request accurately and just pass on the facts, rather than add any spin on the situation.

A few guidelines:

- Make sure everyone in the group has a copy of the prayer chain list with telephone numbers and e-mail addresses.

- Regularly update the list.

- When phoning or e-mailing a prayer request avoid other topics of conversation.

- When taking the call by phone write down the details so you can pass on the correct information.

- Respect people's confidentiality.

- If the person is out when you phone ring the next person on the prayer chain.

- Pray as soon as you can.

9.6   The family connection

How well do I know my wife after over thirty years of marriage? I know everything, from her favorite perfume to her tastes in Indian cuisine. Also, to my shame, I know how to say those choice words that get a reaction: "You're getting just like your mother!" Equally nothing strikes fear and terror into our children more than to be told "I can see your dad in you!" Isn't it strange how we react in such a negative way to these expressions when in truth we are being likened to people we love and respect? Do people see the characteristics of Jesus through us? Is our own prayer life a good example for others? Methods and techniques will help improve the time you spend praying in your homegroups, but I have no doubt the greatest motivation you can bring to the group is to be a living example of someone who spends time with God in prayer. Do others see the family connection between Jesus and you?

9.7 In a nutshell

- There is a difference between praying on your own and praying in a small group.

- Enhance the prayer life of your group by introducing interesting and imaginative ways to pray.

- Don't confuse sharing items for prayer with gossip.

- Don't assume everyone is comfortable praying aloud.

- Develop the prayer life of your group beyond the meeting by introducing a prayer chain.

9.8 Recommended reading

Fuelling the Fire by Dennis Lennon

Prayer: Unwrapping the Gift by John Preston

Multi-Sensory Prayer by Sue Wallace

PART 4:

ORGANIZING HOMEGROUPS

CHAPTER 10

STRUCTURING HOMEGROUPS

10.1 Good organization

Thomas Frederick Cooper is a name that you may not immediately recognize; he was Tommy Cooper, the comedian and magician best known for wearing a fez and his catchphrase, "Just like that." Cooper's style of comedy would not have been considered funny by everyone, as he bumbled through his performances, which appeared to be unrehearsed. Nothing was further from the truth— every joke he told and so-called failed conjuring trick was rehearsed time and time again. He was a master of his profession; a brilliant performer who understood that the success of his act was dependent upon preparation and an eye for detail. He knew nothing happens "just like that."

Jesus also understood there was a time and place for good organization. Imagine the chaos during the miraculous feeding of the five thousand if he had said, "Come and help yourself." How many would have gone hungry or been hurt in the mêlée? How many children would have been pushed out all together? Jesus could have asked the angels to feed the people but instead he told the disciples to organize the crowd into manageable groups of fifty or a hundred. Jesus certainly knew how to be spontaneous and react to the situation around him, he was no control freak, but he also knew when and where it was necessary to organize.

We believe that good organization in the running of homegroups is essential. It is not a case of putting programs and procedures before people but rather a recognition that without them we will not be as effective in caring for the people God has entrusted to us. Don't undervalue good organization; Jesus didn't!

> Then Jesus told the crowd to sit down in groups on the green grass. So they sat in groups of fifty or a hundred. Jesus took the five loaves and two fish, looked up toward heaven, and asked God's blessing on the food. Breaking the loaves into pieces, he kept giving the bread and fish to the disciples to give to the people. (Mark 6:40–41)

10.2 Styles of homegroups

We used to believe that a church homegroup structure should have only one style. Our view is now more flexible, and we are willing to mold around the needs of people. The concept of one-style-fits-all no longer works for many churches that have a wide and diverse congregation with differing needs. It still remains important to keep common goals for groups but at the same time you should be open to encouraging different varieties of homegroups to develop. What are the various options that can be considered?

Geographical location

Another accepted way of arranging homegroups is geographically. This method will usually mean that the groups are made up of a mix of people, both in age and interests. One of the reasons why mixed groups tend to succeed is to do with the breadth of both life experiences and spiritual maturity that help the group to gel.

ADVANTAGES

- It minimizes traveling to homegroups.

- A mix of social backgrounds, age, and interests bring variety and blessing to the group.

- Members may be able to walk to homegroup meetings, allowing those without cars to attend—and be ecologically responsible at the same time!

- It is easier for the group to care for each other practically, easier just to "pop in."

DISADVANTAGES

- It may not necessarily give the best mix of people within the group.

- It may be more difficult to find common interests for social activities.

- Members may want to be with others of their own age.

Common interest groups

These are groups of people with the same interests, which could embrace everything from members of the church worship group to young mothers. A benefit of this style of group is that it enables people to meet at times more suitable to their situations. Groups of this type may be particularly advantageous to those with work commitments who are unable to make a regular midweek group meeting.

ADVANTAGES

- Members share common life situations and support one another.

- They are able to meet at times more suitable to their circumstances.

DISADVANTAGE

- It may mean couples do not attend the same homegroups.

Age groups

Groups structured around age can be most attractive to both ends of the age scale. They appeal to teenagers or those in their early twenties who want to build relationships with their peers. They may also meet the needs of those of retirement age, whose interests and lifestyles are more defined. While groups of this type have benefits, particularly socially, there is the downside that friendships are limited to one age group.

ADVANTAGES

- Share common interests.
- Discuss issues relevant to their age and generation.
- Meet at suitable times/location to fit in with their lifestyle.

DISADVANTAGES

- Lacks spiritual and practical input across the age spectrum.
- Can limit friendships to one's own peer group.

Evangelistic

In these groups, members share a common vision to use their homegroup as an evangelistic witness, somewhere to invite non-Christian partners or friends.

ADVANTAGE

- The group will have a strong sense of purpose and direction.

DISADVANTAGE

- The level of teaching can remain basic.

New Christians

New Christian groups are often established following the completion of an introduction course to the Christian faith. The main advantage of this type of homegroup is that all the members are probably at the same level of spiritual understanding. The benefit of this is that they will feel less intimidated about asking questions and probably already know many of the people in the group. New Christian groups may only run for a short season, as it is can be advisable to move people into established homegroups with mature Christians. Alternatively, those who helped with the course could join the group as well, taking away the need to move people on and making it more likely to hold onto members.

ADVANTAGES

- Relationships already exist.
- They are possibly all at the same spiritual level.

DISADVANTAGES

- The only mature spiritual input is from the leaders.
- Members do not get to know other people within the church by joining an existing homegroup.

Just a thought

This is by no means an exhaustive list of the various styles that could be considered for the structuring of your homegroups. However, what it does is shows us that it is possible for different types of groups to run alongside each other, therefore meeting the total needs of the people that make up your church community.

10.3 Placing people into homegroups

Over the past eighteen months I have become an online shopper, buying everything from fitness equipment to photo frames. What I appreciate most about this style of purchasing is the ability to find what I am looking for quickly, check its availability, and within minutes receive an e-mail confirmation that it is being picked, packed, and on its way. This is convenience shopping at its best! What is the link between Internet shopping and placing people into homegroups? The answer is good service and communication. Having been responsible for allocating people into homegroups for many years, I am a firm believer in the importance of doing this with care, speed, and efficiency. Often a request to join a group is from someone new to the church. It is essential her first impression is of a fellowship concerned enough to place her quickly into a suitable group. Even if your church has only a few homegroups, it is advisable to have some system in place that will ensure the person is allocated to an appropriate group. The more groups you have, the greater the need for procedures. Using an application form for potential group members can be an efficient solution.

Application form

The benefit of using an application form is that it provides those responsible with the information required to place the applicant into an appropriate group. (see following page)

Acknowledge application

Why not copy the online shopping companies, who understand the importance of a quick e-mail response confirming acceptance of an order? It only takes a phone call or e-mail to acknowledge a request to join a homegroup; it all helps to make the applicant feel welcome.

Placement in a suitable homegroup

The information on the application form will prove invaluable in helping to choose an appropriate group. However, it also helps to speak to the person to gain an impression of where you think he would be best placed. The more you know about the person, the easier it will be to

Homegroup Application

I / We are interested in joining a homegroup.

Name(s): _____

Address: _____

Phone: _____

Cell: _____

E-mail: _____

The following information assists in placing
you in an appropriate homegroup.

Age (Please circle):   20s   30s   40s   50s   60+

Marital status: _____

Family (No. of children and ages): _____

Occupation: _____

Previous church (if any): _____

Names of anyone you know in the church: _____

_____

Any additional comments that may be helpful: _____

_____

Signed: _____

Date: _____

Please return the completed form at the Welcome Desk or the Church Office.

Alternatively if you have any questions regarding homegroups
please contact: _____

Phone: _____

E-mail: _____

place him in a homegroup that will meet his needs. It is also important that he should enhance the group they join.

Invitation from homegroup leader

Once the person has been placed in a homegroup, ask the home-group leader to ensure that he is invited to come within two weeks. (See 4.2 Where and when.)

Follow up

After two to three weeks it is advisable to check with the home-group leader that contact has been made and the person is attending the group. No matter how good your systems are and how well-intentioned the leader is, it is not unusual when following up to discover the applicant has not yet been contacted or is not attending. It may be that the leader just needs prompting to make contact, or on the other hand you may be told that the person does not want to attend the proposed group. If this is the case you need to discuss with the applicant in more detail what type of group they are looking for and try to find an appropriate place.

Difficult-to-place people

There will be a few people whose personalities or clinical conditions make it difficult to integrate them into a homegroup. They will not be easy to place and leaders should not be forced to accommodate them as it could have a detrimental effect on the well-being of the group and its leaders. It is advisable not to place a person if you feel it would be unwise to do so, even if the leader is willing to take her. It is important that when a placement has been made it is not viewed as "job done." The leader will need regular follow up and support; otherwise they are likely to feel "dumped on." Ideally everyone is entitled to be in a homegroup but there will always be a very small minority who will never be suited to a small group situation. Do not consider it a failing if you have to accept that not everyone can be placed into a homegroup.

10.4 Homegroup size

Be practical. Is there a limit to the number of people that can be cared for, or how many bodies can be squeezed into a living room? These are issues that require consideration when deciding the ideal size for a homegroup. It is easy to make the mistake of using size as a barometer to determine the well-being of a group. Large groups are not necessarily successful and small ones may not be failing. Some people who may find large groups intimidating will be far more prepared to share and join in a smaller group. You should accept that you all have differing work and family circumstances that will determine how much time can be devoted to being a leader. Leading a homegroup is more than running a midweek Bible study; it is also about fellowship and caring for one another. Wouldn't it be better to have a homegroup of six, properly cared for, than one of eighteen who are not? There is no one size fits all answer; there are many contributing factors that need to be kept in mind when deciding how many people should attend a group. I would suggest that if groups are less than six they are probably too small and over twelve too large; the optimum size is therefore between seven and twelve.

A newspaper article intrigued me about a national bus company who are piloting a scheme where, for a nominal price, you can reserve the seat next to you so no one else can sit there. Is this purely a quirky idea for media attention or have they recognized people need space to enjoy the experience of traveling by bus in order to want to do it again? Admittedly, the person you are sitting next to on the sofa at the homegroup is probably not a stranger, but we all need space. Therefore when determining the number of people that should be assigned to a homegroup it is important firstly to ascertain how many the leader can care for and secondly, the number that can be comfortably seated in the meeting place.

10.5 Why homegroups close

In the evolving life of a church, homegroups will close for a variety of reasons. Perhaps the group was only originally set up with a view that it would run for a short time and has fulfilled its purpose, for example, a new Christian group. Alternatively, it could be that the leaders or even several members of a group are moving from the area and the numbers attending no longer make the group viable. There is also the group that doesn't officially close but goes through a long, lingering, dying process until it eventually fizzles out. Other reasons could include a group where the chemistry between leaders and members does not work.

One thing all these situations have in common is that groups invariably do not reach a point of closure overnight. In the case of leaders moving away they probably have informed you of this months in advance. As for the group that is fizzling out, we would be very surprised if someone has not already made you aware of the situation. What is important is that you do not wait until the last rites have been administered before taking action.

If the leader is moving away, discuss with her or her how best to accommodate the group as soon as possible. As for the group dying on its feet, the signs will have been evident for months; leaders no longer attending training sessions, poor attendance at the meetings, and no one in the group seeming to know what is happening. As the motto of the Boy Scouts says, you should, "Be prepared" for an evolutionary cycle of groups and view this as an opportunity to strengthen your church's homegroup ministry rather than become disillusioned that a group has closed.

There are various reasons why homegroups close. For instance:

Leaders take a break or retire

How long do you expect homegroup leaders to serve: one, two, three years, or indefinitely? For some, length of time is not a problem, as they remain enthusiastic. Can you or should you expect this level of commitment from everyone? It would be good if the answer was yes but in reality you have to acknowledge homegroup leaders can become weary and need a rest from the responsibilities of leadership. Perhaps their circumstances change and they need to step down.

Stepping down or taking a break from leadership does not mean giving up, nor is it an admission of failure. It is a sensible person who recognizes when it is time to recharge her batteries. Leaders should be encouraged to take a break before they burn out or just give up; they are more likely to be willing to take on the responsibility of a new group in the future if they have stopped earlier rather than later.

Leaders may step down for many reasons, including work commitments, pressure of caring for elderly relatives, or simply age. This does not mean they are looking for a back door to escape from their commitments, merely an acknowledgement that their situation has changed and that they can no longer be dedicated to a leadership role as they have been. Usually decisions to step down in these situations do not happen overnight, and the leader invariably sees it as part of his responsibility to ensure that the members of the group are not adversely affected by his decision.

In an ideal world there may be existing members of the group who have the ability and are willing to take over the leadership.

Alternatively, it may be necessary to reallocate the people into other appropriate groups.

Wrong leaders

How do you manage an ineffective group because of the poor placement of a leader? Do you just ignore it or add additional people, hoping this is the remedy? This will probably not resolve the problem and it may require more drastic measures to be taken, such as closing the group and redistributing the members. While this may be a difficult decision to make, experience has shown that in the long term it is best for everyone, including the leader. This needs to be carried out by an appropriate church leader with kindness and honesty. Don't rush the appointment of homegroup leaders; take time to ensure the correct person is selected. (See 11.2 Appointing leaders and 11.4 When it all goes wrong.)

Need for a change

If a group has been together for a long time, some members may simply need a change from the existing leadership style. This is not a reflection on how the group has been run but rather indicates a need for an injection of life.

Leaders or members move away

The dynamics of a group can change when people leave, for example when they are moving away from the area. This particularly affects groups that have a high ratio of people in their twenties to mid-thirties, who are still in a transitory period of their lives. If there are no obvious replacements, it may be the right decision to redistribute the remaining members and close the group.

Members are not compatible

On paper the group looks fine, with good leaders and a nice cross-section of members, but it just doesn't work. Their needs, expectations, and social compatibility simply don't match up. The group may loosely hang together but is unlikely to thrive. It is not an admission of failure to say, "We got this one wrong." Closing and reallocating everyone would serve the group better. This would fall under the responsibility of the homegroup pastors. (See 12.2 What is a homegroup pastor?)

Conflict with other church activities

With busy church programs, choices have to be made. "Do I continue going to homegroup or help lead the children's choir?" Numbers in the group may become depleted for genuine reasons, as people take on other responsibilities within the church. If regular attendance becomes too low, it may be an opportunity to give the leaders a rest and close the group.

10.6 Restructuring homegroups

There is a danger when groups have been together for a long time that they may become stale. Neither the leaders nor members may even be aware of a need for change but would probably benefit by the group being refreshed by dividing. Usually this would only be done if the group has sufficient numbers and there are members of the group who could take on a leadership role. Nevertheless, larger groups with potential leaders should divide to enable the homegroup ministry to grow. Hopefully relationships that have already been established in the previous group will continue and new ones begin. Invariably there will initially be reluctance to do this, especially where friendships have been established. There is also the added benefit of allowing those in a large church to get to know a new group of people.

When dividing a group make sure:

- The group is large enough to divide without adversely affecting its dynamics until new people are added.

- The newly divided groups have sufficient numbers to function effectively and be able to accommodate new people.

- There are those within the group who have the ability and desire to take on a leadership role, ideally having received homegroup leadership training in advance. (See 12.4 Leadership training.)

- Members are reorganized so that they are able to move with people they know, instead of placing them in an environment where they know no one. This will allow the transition to happen more smoothly.

DOs

- Church leaders, with the help of the homegroup leaders, should decide in advance who goes where. Most of us respond to clear direction, but be willing to adjust your plans.

- Gradually introduce the proposed plan to divide the group, which will give people time to embrace the changes.

- Make sure everyone associated with the group is aware of future plans.

- Clearly explain the reason why the group is dividing, helping everyone to understand the benefits both for themselves, the group, and the church.

- Give clear detailed information on when the new groups start, who is in which group, and where they will meet.

- Try to help group members overcome any apprehension.

- Make this a positive move that everyone wants to sign up for.

- Once implemented, meet up with the other group for a social get-together so that friendships can be maintained. It may be a nice idea to keep an on-going association with the previous group. This will help reassure everyone that socially they will still stay in touch with friends from their former homegroup.

DON'Ts

- Don't spring the change onto the group without prior warning.

- Don't assume everyone will be happy with these new arrangements immediately; we all adjust to change at a different pace.

- Don't rush through this change.

Just a thought

Remember that you are dealing with individuals who will not always agree with your proposals. For most of us change does not come easily as we like to remain in our comfort zones, so any reorganization of homegroups needs to be handled with care. It is all too easy for a great idea to go "pear shaped." Not everyone will see this as a benefit and may even use the opportunity as a "get out of jail (homegroup)" card! Encourage the group leader and the members to see this as dividing to grow for the Kingdom rather than having to give up their group. These dos and don'ts are only suggestions; you know your groups better than anyone.

10.7 Group attendance

At least twice a year a review of who is attending or associated with each homegroup should be carried out. This will enable both the group leaders and those overseeing the homegroup ministry to assess the well-being of the groups. Keep the process simple as you are looking for the big picture answer. Three questions to be asked are:

- Who attends the group regularly? Include those who attend every meeting and are actively involved in the group.

- Who attends irregularly? Include those who consider themselves members of the group, even though they don't attend every meeting.

- Who is associated with the group? Include those who consider themselves to be associated with the group even though they are unable to attend.

This regular reviewing of homegroups will prove to be invaluable as it provides factual information of actual attendance on a regular basis. More importantly, it will identify any who have stopped attending the group and may require follow up.

There may be a group that has a high number of people associated with it but only a few who attend on a regular basis. However, do not jump to conclusions that the group is dysfunctional; it is advisable to consider the following questions:

- Is the group achieving a sense of community?

- Why are people not attending?

After review, it may turn out that the concerns are ill-founded as the group is functioning well and the leaders are to be commended for their care. The reason for the low regular attendance is the individual circumstances of the group members and not a reflection on the group leadership. Alternatively, it may show that the group has problems and the leaders require additional support and encouragement.

10.8 In a nutshell

- Don't undervalue good organization; Jesus didn't.

- Different styles of homegroups should fit comfortably alongside each other.

- When placing people into homegroups do so with care, speed, and efficiency.

- The number of people in a homegroup has more to do with how many the leaders can care for rather than the size of their house.

- Look out for signs of an ailing homegroup before it becomes terminal.

- When reorganizing homegroups think people first, procedures second.

- Regularly evaluate group attendance.

10.9 Recommended reading

How to Build a Small Groups Ministry by Neal F. McBride

How to Lead Small Groups by Neal F. McBride

CHAPTER 11

QUALITIES OF A LEADER

11.1 Shepherd leaders

My training in leadership began when I was fourteen—not by reading books or attending seminars but by simply observing my church youth leaders. I was privileged to be part of a youth group run by men with leadership qualities.

Martyn was the enthusiast and visionary. Alfred and Albert faithfully taught God's word, always prepared and able to answer the questions of skeptical teenagers, while Bob brought order in a fun way.

As my responsibility in leadership has increased, I now appreciate how much time and effort these faithful men of God put into their youth work. One of my treasured memories is a mystery outing they organized for the youth group. Even forty years later I can still vividly recall Alfred's retelling of the story of David and Goliath. It must have taken him hours of preparation to ensure we hung onto his every word. Bob, who is now in his late eighties, faithfully attends church and greets me with a firm handshake. We enjoy reminiscing about those special days in the youth group. Bob would be embarrassed if I described him as one of my leadership role models, as he is a modest man who would simply say, "I did nothing special." Looking back over many years I have met few people with the leadership skills of Martyn, Alfred, Albert, and Bob. Their abilities were not only obtained from textbooks but were learned from following the example of a true servant leader, Jesus.

Jesus spoke to people in ways they would understand, using everyday illustrations from the harvesting of crops to the sights and sounds of the shepherds on the hillsides caring for their sheep. Probably everyone would have heard stories about the local shepherds and their acts of courage while protecting their flock—even if the tale had become exaggerated over the years! Shepherds were known for the leading and caring of their sheep.

A good shepherd would:

- Find clear and fresh drinking water for his sheep.

- Look for new grazing pastures.

- Care for his sheep day and night.

- Know each sheep individually.

- Lead rather than drive his sheep.

- Look for any sheep that got lost or into difficulty.

The qualities of a homegroup leader should be similar to those of a shepherd.

A homegroup leader should:

- Make God's word clear and refreshing.
- Care for those within their homegroup.
- Know their group individually.
- Lead rather than drive.
- Follow up on any who drift away.

I find it reassuring that Jesus chose twelve ordinary men to be his apostles or "messengers," not for their outstanding ability as leaders but simply because they had a willingness to follow him. One heard the teaching of Jesus but did not love and obey him, and eleven gave it everything, even if at times they got it horribly wrong.

As long as our heart and attitudes are right, Jesus can use us. You should never forget it is only by God's grace that you can truly love and care for each other or have that desire to lead a Bible study with a passion that will make it more than mere words.

11.2 Appointing leaders

Before appointing a leader the following question needs to be considered: "Do they have the necessary leadership and pastoral care qualities to be a good homegroup leader?" Not everyone has the gifting to be a leader and their style and personality may not work in a small group environment.

Some of the most effective group leaders are quiet, gentle people who would never describe themselves as leadership material. There is no better example of a quiet, reluctant leader than Moses who protested to God, "I don't have the qualities you are looking for" (Exodus 3 and 4). Natural leadership ability is a plus for leading a group, but you should not overlook the importance of God-given qualities. What then are the characteristics you should look for in a leader?

Characteristics of a homegroup leader

SPIRITUAL

- Christian maturity
- Growth in his or her own faith
- Desire to see the group grow spiritually
- Desire to pray with and for members of the group

CARE AND CONCERN

- Sensitivity to the needs of the group and individuals
- Enjoyment of serving and encouraging other people
- Provision of practical care and support

ORGANIZATIONAL

- Ability to prepare and lead a Bible study
- Ability to encourage participation
- Ability to lead without dominating

Try to avoid making a hurried decision when selecting homegroup leaders. From our own experience, a poor appointment invariably results in a dysfunctional group. Even worse is when the leader believes he is doing a great job and everyone in the group is crying, "Get me out of here!" There are no guarantees and errors of judgment will occasionally happen when appointing leaders. However, there are a few guidelines that will help in the decision making process.

Guidelines for appointing leaders

- Plan ahead for new homegroups and identify potential new leaders.

- Do not make hasty leader appointments.

- Avoid making appointments without discussing with other church leaders first.

- Ask the existing homegroup leaders if there are people within their group who would make good leaders in the future.

- Present the names to the church leaders for any additional input. This will prove to be invaluable as the homegroup leaders may not be fully aware of an individual's situation or whether they are being considered for another role within the fellowship.

- Discuss possible new appointments with the homegroup pastors. (See 12.2 What is a homegroup pastor?)

- Talk to potential leaders about the possibility of their becoming homegroup leaders.

- Allow people time to think and pray about this responsibility.

- Invite them to attend a homegroup leader's training session. (See 12.4 Leadership training.)

- If they are already attending a homegroup, keep their leaders informed.

- Follow up but don't force a decision.

The sole leader

It is not advisable for someone to lead a group on his or her own. This is not to imply that only married couples make suitable leaders—two single people could be equally effective. But it is important for leaders to have someone alongside them to share both the blessings and the responsibilities of leadership. There is a greater risk that the homegroup will suffer under a sole leader, who has total responsibility for everything, from providing care to organizing social activities. Admittedly if the leader has good organizing ability, tasks can be delegated, but it is a blessing to know that someone stands alongside you in leadership. We all need someone with whom we can share confidential problems and who will cheer us up when the group is getting us down.

11.3 Homegroup leaders: a job description

Is it really necessary to have a job description for leaders? I consider it to be crucial. There is security in knowing what responsibilities are expected in homegroup leadership. From my experience people view a job description as reassurance rather than a threat.

Draft Job Description:

Role title: *Homegroup leader* Responsible to: *Homegroup pastor*

Overall purpose of role

The primary role of the homegroup leader is to support and encourage members within their homegroup through Bible study, prayer, and fellowship.

Key tasks

- To oversee the organization of the homegroup meeting, i.e. appropriate meeting time and venue.

- To lead the homegroup or to ensure it is led by a competent member of the homegroup.

- To be willing to add new members to the homegroup and encourage their integration.

- To meet regularly with homegroup pastors.

- To ensure that an appropriate amount of time is given to fellowship, Bible study, and prayer on a homegroup evening.

- To use the provided study notes in line with other homegroups.

- To provide care and support to members within the homegroup.

- To be an encourager of the church community.

- To be part of the homegroup prayer chain.

- To support and encourage spiritual growth and discernment, both individually and to the group as a whole.

Pastoral care

It is also important to provide pastoral care and support for members within the homegroup. If issues arise that are outside the homegroup leader's realm, he or she should advise the homegroup pastor or the appropriate leader within the church.

Other tasks

- To oversee the organization of social events within the homegroup as and when appropriate.

- To attend homegroup leaders' meetings.

- To attend homegroup leaders' training.

11.4 When it all goes wrong

One of the most difficult situations in the overseeing of home-groups is when an established group becomes dysfunctional because of poor leadership. This is not necessarily because the wrong leaders were chosen in the first place, but could simply be their life circumstances make it difficult for them to meet the requirements of homegroup leadership. For instance, changes in their employment can mean they can no longer lead and care for the group to the standard required. Some leaders will reach the point of accepting for themselves that it is time to take a break and step down from leadership, recognizing it is the right decision for them and the group. Although this will undoubtedly cause some disruption while a new leader is appointed or members are redistributed to other groups, hopefully everything can be done amicably.

The more difficult problem is when the leader does not recognize that it is time to relinquish his or her leadership responsibilities. How then do you handle this situation—a leader who is reluctant to let go but whose group is failing? Some might suggest doing nothing and the situation will inevitably resolve itself. Eventually people will stop attending and the group will naturally close. We do not believe this is fair, for either the members of the group or the leader. Some form of action will be necessary.

We do not have a one sentence answer to the question just raised. Knowing what to do is one thing; how to do it is something altogether different. After all, homegroups are about caring for people, and that has to include the leaders. These are just our thoughts, but that is all they can be—every situation is different. We are in the job of building up people rather than knocking them down. However the situation is handled, it has to be with love and sensitivity, and it must be done in a non-judgmental way. For your encouragement and from our own experiences of dealing with individuals, both secularly and in the church, when you get alongside and explain your concerns, deep down, people will realize what you are sharing is true. You may be surprised that what you thought was going to be a difficult encounter turns out more positively. The leaders may well be willing to talk things through, as they are relieved that someone has recognized they are struggling. We cannot guarantee every time you have a situation of this nature that it will end like a romantic Harlequin romance novel where everyone is happy. The fact is some people may not take kindly to what you are suggesting: that they should either step down from leadership or they require support. You may have to accept, for the sake of the members of the group, the right decision has been taken to approach the leader, even if she is unhappy about the way she considers you have handled it. We would advise before any contact is made the situation is discussed and prayed about with the leadership of the church, as it cannot be the responsibility of one person.

Just a thought

Do we allow the media to shape our opinions on leadership? We see politicians making the headlines, not always for the right reasons, the soccer manager who has been banned from the touchline, or the boss who is only concerned about his own ego. Strong, forceful leadership is not necessarily wrong but probably does not suit homegroups. Jesus gave us a strong example that was not in a pushy, forceful way. He showed what it meant to be a servant leader when he humbled himself to wash the feet of the disciples. This was an act of meekness, but at the same time, he remained secure in who he was, the Son of God.

> Whoever wants to be a leader among you must be your
> servant, and whoever wants to be first must be the slave
> of all. For even I, the Son of Man, came here not to be

served but to serve others, and to give my life as a ransom for many. (Mark 10:43–45)

11.5 In a nutshell

- You cannot go wrong if you use Jesus as your role model of a leader.

- It can be a lonely responsibility being a sole leader of a group.

- Poor leadership assignments are far easier to get into than to get out of!

- To be a leader you first have to know how to be a servant.

11.6 Recommended reading

Servant Leadership by J. David Lundy

The 21 Irrefutable Laws of Leadership by John C. Maxwell

Developing the Leader Within You by John Maxwell

CHAPTER 12

SUPPORTING LEADERS

12.1 Caring for your leaders

Following the marriage of our daughter, Lizzie, it was fascinating the number of people who made the remark that we were fortunate to have our children off our hands. We know what they meant by this expression, but did they really think our parenting days were over? It is true we no longer drop the children off at youth group, but instead we are asked to baby-sit or help with decorating. Did we ever really think once they celebrated their eighteenth birthday, we could wave them off at the front door and then celebrate a job well-done with a glass of champagne? Our role as parents never ends; it perpetually changes as they will always be our children who require our love and support. Is there a similarity between parenting and looking after homegroup leaders? We would emphatically say yes. It is not enough just to appoint people as homegroup leaders and then wave them off from the steps of the church and then say "job well-done." Homegroup leaders will equally need support and care in the same way they care for the members of their group.

This reminds me of a phone call from Mark, a pastor I know through my work with homegroups. He called to share with me a difficult situation that had arisen with one of his group leaders. Mark recounted that he had received a visit from the leader who was angry and at the point of resigning. The gist of the story is that John and his wife, Judith, were running a difficult and complex group of people that they had worked with for several years. Despite having asked for help on numerous occasions nothing had been done to provide the extra support they required. They had reached a point where they had decided there was only one course of action and that was to quit.

I tried to give Mark a few ideas of how he might resolve the situation both in the short and long term. However, from what he had told me it would appear that in his church structure there was no one who had direct responsibility to care for the homegroup leaders. This equally meant that leaders who had a problem had no one other than Mark, the pastor, to turn to for support and advice. My recommendation to him was that he should consider introducing homegroup pastors as a way of caring for the leaders.

12.2 What is a homegroup pastor?

Don't get sidetracked by the term "homegroup pastor." It is not the title that is important but the role. Perhaps a more appropriate title would be coach. It gives a sense of getting alongside, supporting and encouraging rather than being the boss. A coach would be a person who is a mentor, adviser, guide, and also a motivator. Essential as these attributes are for any form of leadership, the homegroup pastor also needs to have spiritual qualities including wisdom, discernment, and a calling from God to this position.

How might a homegroup pastor have supported Mark, Judith, and John? It was unrealistic to expect Mark, as the pastor, to be the receiver for every situation and problem that arose from the groups. He therefore needed to have people in place that could take on the responsibilities of overseeing and organizing the homegroups but more importantly to provide the pastoral care and support for the leaders. This is not a fail-safe system and inevitably problems will still arise. However, the group leaders now have someone to turn to for support. Similarly, the pastor knows that an important part of the life of his church is being cared for on a day-by-day basis.

What are the qualities of a homegroup pastor?

We are not in favor of the philosophy one-size-fits-all and therefore want to avoid putting the qualities of a homegroup pastor into a straitjacket. All of us have different abilities and gifts. However, there are some essential requirements for a homegroup pastor:

- To be assured of God's calling.
- To be mature in his or her faith.
- To have a pastoral heart for people.
- To be an active member of the church.
- To have had experience as a homegroup leader.
- To have leadership qualities.
- To have sufficient time available to fulfill the role.

Quite rightly, being a mature Christian, having a pastoral heart for people, and a sense of God's calling are at the top of the list. It is also important not to skip over the last point regarding time. It is wise not to appoint someone as a homegroup pastor who has all the attributes but doesn't have sufficient time to fulfill the role because of work, family, or other church commitments. Choosing someone without enough time is likely to cause frustration on everyone's part. The homegroup pastor will be aware he is not fulfilling his responsibilities to the best of his abilities, and the leaders will not feel they are being cared for in the way they should be. On a more light-hearted note, there are two other qualities that haven't quite made it onto the list but help to make good homegroup pastors: a sense of humor to share in the fun of homegroups and a healthy appetite as inevitably every group will want to invite you to their barbecue!

The number of homegroup pastors required will depend on the number of groups in the church. My recommendation is that a homegroup pastor should not have responsibility for more than four or five groups. This may not seem like many, but if you assume an average group has two leaders and at least six members, this adds up to between forty and fifty people, which is more than enough for a homegroup pastor to be responsible for. Also do not overlook the fact that homegroup pastors need support and encouragement, and it is important that they are part of a homegroup even if they cannot regularly attend.

It is worth considering having homegroup pastors work in teams; married couples are ideally suited to take on the role. This should not exclude single people from becoming homegroup pastors, but there is merit in having a male/female team. Perhaps we are being overcautious in this area but we do consider there are some situations that require same-sex input.

The provision of homegroup pastors may not necessarily meet the needs of your church. Nevertheless, the basic principle that leaders and their groups will require ongoing care and attention does not change.

Just a thought

It doesn't take a professional landscaper to tell us that for our garden to look in top condition throughout the year it will require regular maintenance. From the first cutting of the grass in early spring to the raking up of leaves in the Fall the work has to be ongoing. It goes without saying, the larger the garden the more time it takes. Hopefully, we are not stretching this analogy too far when we say that homegroup leaders are not vastly different; they also require regular care and nurturing throughout the year. This is the role of the homegroup pastor.

12.3 Homegroup pastor's job description

Role title: *Homegroup pastor*

Responsible to: *Church leadership*

Responsible for: *Homegroup leaders under their responsibility*

Overall purpose of role

The primary role is to provide pastoral care and support for homegroup leaders.

Key tasks

- To meet with their homegroup leaders at least once every term to encourage them and identify areas of need and action.

- To meet socially with homegroup leaders.

- To meet regularly with designated church leaders for planning and vision meetings.

- To organize training for homegroup leaders.

- To organize a prayer chain.

- To organize homegroup leaders meetings.

- To visit the homegroups as and when possible.

- To be an encourager of the church community.

- To support and encourage spiritual growth and discernment within the homegroups.

- To allocate new people into homegroups.

- To appoint new leaders.

- To oversee the selection or preparation of Bible study notes.

- To provide pastoral care and support for homegroup leaders. If issues arise that are outside the homegroup pastor's scope, to advise the appropriate leader within the church.

12.4 Leadership training

On a cold, wet Sunday morning in April we stood on the pavement in the Docklands watching athletes run the London Marathon. We were there with friends to encourage our son, Simon, who was running for the first time. The last race he had competed in was at his primary school sports day twenty years earlier—a slight exaggeration! Simon would not consider himself an athlete even though he regularly works out and had trained for the race. His goals before the race were just to participate and finish; the time was unimportant. We would suspect the majority of the thirty-six thousand runners taking part shared the same ambition—simply to complete the race.

Hopping on and off the Tube, we followed the route of the race cheering the runners as the miles counted down. We saw Simon go by at the nine and the eighteen milemarkers, still in good physical shape, before we made our way to the finishing line. Crowds gathered at Horse Guards Parade to congratulate the triumphant runners, husbands waiting for their wives, children for their dads. The faces of the runners glowed with a cocktail of pride and exhaustion as they showed off their medals. Just taking part was no longer good enough, completing the race and attaining an impressive time was now the real achievement. Simon will proudly show you his medal and then add, "I finished the race in four hours, thirty-four minutes, twenty-six seconds." Every second counts!

Just as training is essential for the marathon runner so is training essential for the homegroup leader. We accept there are those who are naturally gifted as leaders and can take on the responsibility more easily. This, however, is not true for the majority, and therefore training is important for anyone in homegroup leadership. Ideally, homegroup leaders should receive some form of training before being appointed. We do realize, however, that if this rule were stringently applied, many groups would be leaderless. But the organizers of homegroups should consider training necessary, not only for existing leaders but also for potential leaders. It is all too easy to wrongly presume that people instinctively know how to prepare and lead a Bible study or lead prayer in a small group setting. Admittedly people are learning all the time by observing others but there is no substitute for formal training where good practices can be taught and learned.

One form of training is "mentor" training; this is forward thinking training, identifying people who have the potential to be future leaders. It is allowing them an opportunity to "have a go" at leading in the safety of their homegroup with the support of the main group leaders. For example, when leading the Bible study they are secure in the knowledge that there is a safety net in the form of their mentor leader if they begin to choke up.

Another form of training is through workshops, and it may well be possible for you to organize your own. Look around at the leaders you have, and then calculate how many years of experience they have of running homegroups. You will probably be surprised at the wealth of potential trainers in leadership you have at your disposal. We attend regular training sessions at our church, led by the homegroup pastors. These are relaxed and informal sessions that usually begin with breakfast and cover a wide diversity of topics from how to care for your group to leading a Bible study. These sessions are an opportunity to invite potential leaders so they can gain experience. The word training may seem intimidating to some people, therefore every effort is taken to ensure that at no time will anyone be embarrassed, everything taught is achievable, and that the whole experience is positive.

The following is a draft outline of a training program we have used:

8:30–9:15	Breakfast of donuts and juice
9:15–9:30	Worship
9:30–9:45	Jesus' view on caring for people
9:45–10:30	Handling confidential issues
10:30–11:00	Coffee
11:00–11:30	How to improve our listening skills
11:30–12:15	How to handle criticism
12:15–12:30	Closing prayer and worship

Just by reading this book your training has already begun but please don't stop there. Why not organize for your church to run a training session for the leaders, either led by competent people within your own fellowship or by outside trainers? It would be time and money well-invested.

Just a thought

A postscript to Simon running the London Marathon: he recently ran the Heritage half marathon in South Africa. (It's a mystery why he wanted to run as he was on his honeymoon!) Simon had not prepared for this race and although he finished with a good time, he was unable to walk for the next few days. He had forgotten that no matter how fit you think you are, training is essential for a race. Just as training for the marathon runner is necessary, so is training for the homegroup leader. You should never consider the task complete. Everyone can benefit from training, no matter how long they have been homegroup leaders.

12.5 In a nutshell

- Do not presume leaders are self-sufficient; all of them require support and encouragement.

- A homegroup pastor should be a mentor, adviser, guide, and motivator.

- All of us can benefit from training no matter how long we have been homegroup leaders.

- Begin the training of tomorrow's leaders today.

A PERSONAL CONCLUSION FROM THE TWO OF US

We would be less than honest if we did not say that the writing of this book has given us some difficult moments. We now know what is meant by writers' block! The problem has not been what to write but rather conveying it in a readable and accessible style.

Having overcome the writing problem, there was still one more personal challenge—"Do we live up to the standards of homegroup leadership that we have written about?" To be honest with you, there were more than a few occasions that our response was, "No, we do not." Although we have been involved in the leadership of homegroups for many years, we still consider that we have a great deal to learn, or in some cases re-learn. We would be embarrassed if you got the impression that we were the finished articles, as far as homegroup leadership is concerned. Together we have written this book as honestly as we know how. Hopefully the practical insights and stories will resonate with you. Above all else our prayer is that having read this book, you are encouraged in your homegroup ministry.

> Unless the Lord builds a house, the work of the builders is useless. (Psalm 127:1)

Your co-homegroup leaders

Steve & Mandy Briars